KNOWING
AS MOVING

KNOWING AS MOVING

PERCEPTION, MEMORY, AND PLACE

SUSAN LEIGH FOSTER

Duke University Press   Durham and London   2025

© 2025 Duke University Press
This work is licensed under a Creative Commons Attribution-NonCommercial-NoDerivatives 4.0 International License.
Project Editor: Lisa Lawley
Typeset in Whitman Text and Trade Gothic LT Std
by Copperline Book Services

Library of Congress Cataloging-in-Publication Data
Names: Foster, Susan Leigh, author
Title: Knowing as moving : perception, memory, and place / Susan Leigh Foster.
Description: Durham : Duke University Press, 2025. | Includes bibliographical references and index.
Identifiers: LCCN 2024050925 (print)
LCCN 2024050926 (ebook)
ISBN 9781478032144 (paperback)
ISBN 9781478028901 (hardcover)
ISBN 9781478061106 (ebook)
Subjects: LCSH: Dance—Psychological aspects. | Movement, Psychology of. | Body language. | Mind and body. | Human beings—Attitude and movement. | Self-consciousness (Awareness)
Classification: LCC GV1588.5 .F678 2025 (print) | LCC GV1588.5 (ebook) | DDC 306.4/846—dc23/eng/20250210
LC record available at https://lccn.loc.gov/2024050925
LC ebook record available at https://lccn.loc.gov/2024050926

ISBN 9781478094500 (ebook/other)

Cover art: Photograph by Gilbert B. Weingourt

This book is freely available in an open access edition thanks to the generous support of the University of California Libraries.

To my dear friends

CONTENTS

SETTING OUT BY LOOKING BACK · ix

ESSAYING · 1
WALKING AS PLACE-MAKING · 13
BEING, KNOWING, AND ACTING · 36
EMBODYING THE DECOLONIAL · 56
REMEMBERING DANCING · 78
DANCING'S AFFORDANCES · 97

CONTINUING ON . . . · 121

NOTES · 123
BIBLIOGRAPHY · 139
INDEX · 151

SETTING OUT BY LOOKING BACK

This book began on a walk I was taking in which I looked across at a path I no longer walked and suddenly remembered with startling clarity an encounter with an elderly couple I often saw there. The woman gestured proudly toward a young but very sturdy live oak tree next to us and told me that she had planted it there forty years earlier. Why, I thought, did I suddenly remember this conversation from years earlier? Why, I asked myself, standing here, did I remember something I hadn't thought of for years?

I started reading and continued walking.

Long a fan of James J. Gibson's work on kinesthesia, I wondered whether my physical location and actions might have prompted the memory. I was very surprised to discover how his work has been taken up by a new generation of cognitive scientists approaching the study of a mind in a radically new way. I read unsystematically and unguided through their studies, all the while sustaining my interest in Native philosophy and Native fiction. Native novelists created overlapping worlds that facilitated my understanding of Native philosophy, and the philosophers, in turn, deepened my appreciation of the marvelous ways that the fiction writers crafted similar concepts and ideas. With the neuroscience, I studied footnotes, trying to ascertain who was arguing what. One author led to another, but it was messy.

Friends and colleagues made recommendations. Folders of notes with various titles such as "Intercorporeality," "Relationality," "Memory," "Tongva history," "Cognitive Science," "Conquest," "Disability," and "Indigeneity," emerged. I was very fortunate to have the assistance of highly capable graduate student researchers during this time who dumped massive amounts of reading into these folders. L. Archer Porter, Jackie Davis, Zena Bibler, Laura Smith, and Cora Miller Laszlo, all outstanding scholars in their own right, I thank you from the bottom of my heart.

Unlike my last book, *Valuing Dance*, where I built a machine and systematically processed dance through it, the meandering I was doing for this project seemed to hold very little coherence. Eventually, islands with very fuzzy shores started to appear. Fine, I thought, let it be a collection of essays.

Then I started talking about it with my dear friend and butt-buster walking partner, Alex Purves. Her questions and comments helped a lot. Then I sent it out to Anurima Banerji, Clare Croft, Jacqueline Shea Murphy, and Tria Blu Wakpa, none of whom said not to do it and all of whom gave me great advice. Jacqueline, in particular, pushed back on some of my assumptions, and I'm very grateful to her for it. Lionel Popkin subsequently reviewed rewritten portions of the manuscript, and his comments were also deeply insightful. Thank you all.

Five rewrites in, I send the manuscript to Diana Taylor, who forwards it to Ken Wissoker. Thank you, Diana. Ken, who has been spot-on throughout this whole process, advises me to rewrite it before he sends it out to readers, which I do. Thank you, Ken. And now, I've rewritten it again, thanks to the extraordinarily supportive yet critical and deeply insightful feedback from two anonymous readers. I am profoundly grateful to you both. You couldn't have given me a more generous gift. Finally, I thank the project editor, Lisa Lawley, and copyeditor, Valerie Paquin.

So, the process of bringing this book into the world has been a long one, and I worry that many of my references are dated. Still, the rewrites gave me opportunities to mull over what I and the others I'm engaging with are saying. I have sat with it, walked with it, danced with it.

KNOWING
AS MOVING

ESSAYING

Why do accounts of dancing endlessly assert that "the body is an instrument of or vehicle for expression" and that it "must be subjected to rigorous discipline," or that "intensive practice leads to freedom"? Why do they explain dancing as "executing an idea" or "responding to an inner necessity"? Why do dancers talk about something called "muscle memory," "bodily wisdom," "blood memory," or "the body's knowledge as different from the mind"? Why do their teachers issue instructions like "Your arm should be here," "Push harder and lift higher," "Keep your foot perpendicular to the floor"? Why do my students point to their head when they mention thinking while envisioning the rest of their body responding to that thinking?

The acts of dancing and learning to dance lay bare epistemological assumptions underlying partitions constructed between mind and body. Particularly in Euro-American concert dance and in university and private studio classes, the practice of dancing continually relies on descriptions of who is doing what to whom, and the vast preponderance of these center on the presumption that something "mental" tells the "physical" what to do, or, alternatively, that the physical takes over and spontaneously and uncontrollably does what it wants. Corollary to this mind-body division of labor is the understanding that perception is a passive intake of "stimuli," and response is an active and often physical reaction. Thus, in all the phrases quoted in this essay's first paragraph, the body as instrument comes into being as a result of the assumption that an idea needs to be expressed and that to express this "idea," the body must be continually and methodically drilled to attain virtuoso capabilities. Yet in the development of those technical capacities, dancers begin to experience a reservoir of knowing they label "bodily knowledge," while at the same time being unable to imagine that all knowledge might be physical and that all "ideas" might involve proprioceptive sensations.

In an effort to expose and contest the underlying assumptions reflected in the questions listed in the opening of this essay, and from a somatically based interface with my surroundings, I am reaching out into foreign lands: moving into them while endeavoring to be a respectful guest.[1] As a dancer and dance scholar, I enter spaces and territories formed by other disciplines' scholarship, and as part of my practice of attempting to read nonextractively, I spend time trying to live with an argument or idea, physicalizing it and reflecting on how it moves me. I also ask myself, "How is the author's body moving?" or "How does the writing move toward me?" Sometimes, an idea seems to take hold; other times, I am sure I have grasped it, but I have not. Throughout this process the only constant is the mindful body's continual change.

. . .

The essays bound together in this volume examine how bodies engage in the actualizing of connectedness.[2] Unified by the assertion that knowing takes place through bodily movement, they variously consider the act of moving in and through the world in its potentiality to unite, commune, remember, and make place. Identifying strong resonances among certain scholars in Indigenous and Native studies,[3] ecological cognitive science, disability studies, phenomenology, and new materialism, these essays explore how knowledge is neither static nor storable.[4] These scholars also undertake, in different ways, a critique of mind-body duality. By focusing on the centrality of bodily movement in their arguments, I intend to contribute to decolonial studies a critique of Cartesian dualism and the colonizing politics it enacts.[5]

Colonization, settler colonialism, and neo-imperialism have been extensively analyzed in terms of the ways they claim and control both land and all the living beings that inhabit it.[6] Although different interpretations of the term are widespread, with many arguing that land repatriation is its central goal, a substantial number of scholars are using *decolonization* to reference many diverse processes that address epistemic justice, albeit with less tangible consequences for land redistribution.[7] In alignment with this use of the term and drawing primarily on the work of Enrique Dussel (Argentine-Mexican), Ramón Grosfoguel (Puerto Rican), and Sylvia Wynter (Jamaican),[8] this book examines the mind's colonial status over the body, proposing that mind-body duality is saturated with many of the same relationships—procedures of dominance and control, claims of hierarchically based superiority, and the unruliness and rebelliousness of the subjugated. Each of these essays, by engaging with multiple different bodies of scholarship, explores the structurings of power that define mind-body dualism and undertakes to suggest alternative conceptions of what thinking is by asserting theorizations of connectedness.

What does connectedness feel like? The answer proposed by the neuroscientists and phenomenologists considered in this volume is that it is so intrinsic that it is often barely sensed, and yet it is continual and constant. Connectedness is the product of moving while registering both the proprioceptive and sensory information that movement produces. The fact that this simple process occurs at the interface between body and surroundings sutures them together, or as some would argue, establishes their fundamental unity. Is it because of my experience as a dancer that I feel more easily able to access what these texts are describing as the way that moving produces perception? Dancing, like many other movement-focused activities, can bring awareness of connectedness with the world into consciousness because it directs attention to the proprioceptive information that movement produces, whether through the acts of receiving instruction about what to attend to or copying another's movement. Although for many periods of the day I lose that awareness, what these scientists are claiming about how movement creates connectedness offers me insight that I feel bone deep.

Connectedness, however, is not merely an individual experience. As many Native scholars argue, it extends across the entire human and other-than-human world. In his book *Research Is Ceremony*, Shawn Wilson (Opaskwayak Cree) outlines Indigenous approaches to research among Native peoples in Canada and Australia, arguing that relationships do not shape but rather constitute reality.[9] Lauren Tynan (Pairrebenne Trawlwoolway) expands on what this might mean, by offering the example of two possible answers to the question "How is the river related to the mountain?"[10] One answer sees both the mountain and the river as part of nature. The other observes that the river flows down the mountain. The first answer, she argues, conducts a standard classificatory procedure by looking for the likeness between the two in terms of how they are the same, whereas the second answer considers the relationship they have to one another—that is, their kinship. It is this second approach, for which she advocates in conducting research that is reciprocal, respectful, and willing to consider all beings and entities as variously in relation and connected.

Leanne Betasamosake Simpson (Michi Saagiig Nishnaabeg) argues that connectedness both reveals itself and is built through patient observation and quiet attentiveness. It is then reaffirmed in choices made throughout one's daily life as well as in ceremonial contexts.[11] In addition to observation and patience, according to Simpson, an Indigenous approach to building connection requires creativity in devising contact with what one is observing so that a bond that is "based on mutual respect, reciprocity, and caring" can be forged.[12] This connection must sustain and promote all life, rather than privileging some life over other life.[13] As Simpson details, an Indigenous approach to world-making focuses on alignment with rather than domination over, and it promotes a willingness to decenter human superiority.[14] It also encourages a constant repositioning of oneself as a learner. Further, it validates bodily experience as a potential reservoir of knowledge.

In her essay "Land as Pedagogy," Simpson elaborates further on how connectedness as kinship is developed by detailing the process through which a young Native girl, whose curiosity is supported by the community, pays close attention to her surroundings. As a result of that attentiveness, she discovers the deliciousness of maple sap. This process, as Simpson explains, entails first watching a squirrel eat the sap, tasting it herself, and then telling others who trust and support her exploration. Reading Simpson's description, I try to imagine the girl's attentiveness—her quiet alertness, intense focus, slight shifts of head and body, and a continual energizing of her stance that stretches in the direction of the squirrel. The squirrel the young girl is watching senses the texture of the bark, the pull of gravity, and the smell of sap through its movements, just as the sap itself knows the vigor of the tree and the warming temperature as it begins to travel. The girl's subtle changes in posture reaffirm her relation to the squirrel as she remains both strongly directed yet calm, so that the squirrel senses that she is not a threat. She also takes in the temperature and air currents, sounds of other creatures in the forest, and the changing light. Her physical energy, motion, and restraint undergird her understanding of all that is in relation in those moments.

These essays are similarly the result of watching and copying, observing, and translating movements into words. They are also the product of reading, pausing, assimilating, and digesting, and then seeking interaction with others to determine the validity of my interpretation. What if reading is not that different from observing a squirrel and tasting the maple sap it has nibbled? What if an idea is apprehended by taking it in and trying it out, assimilating it into one's body and putting it into action? And what if the taking in of an idea and the trying it out both consist of bodily action? These are some of the questions this set of essays addresses in an effort to explore how moving produces knowing.

Not only does movement yield knowledge, it forms the basis of what is known at any given moment in time. Yes, knowledge resides in dances, ceremonies, and other rituals, but it is only known during the enacting of these rituals. Similarly, the knowledge lodged in archives and museums is only transformed into knowing through the actions of people as they seek it out. As I will argue throughout this volume, thinking is a physical action, the product of an entire neuromuscular system with its mobile postural and gestural configurations, perceptual systems, and brain activity. Reading, exploring, examining, talking, and remembering are all forms of moving, and any processes of thinking and knowing include some kind of physical action to establish both one's identity and one's relationality. Rather than Descartes's "I think, and therefore I am," the scholars discussed here might argue, "I move, and therefore I know."

Simpson additionally reminds readers that the girl's learning takes place within an environment that is supportive of her inquiries. She emphasizes that when curiosity and investigation occur in an environment that is authoritarian, dismissive, rigid, and judgmental, they will not yield any learning. Contrasting Native conceptions of discovering and learning with settler-colonial attitudes toward knowledge extraction, she highlights the communal nature of coming to know as well as the processual quality of learning as a series of interactions. Her entire community supports the young girl's explorations as part of their shared understanding of the world. Simpson's story thus offers both an indictment and rejection of settler-colonial values and a validation of Native ways of knowing.

Contemplating Simpson's story, I reflect on my own community and learning contexts. On the one hand, I have enjoyed a highly supportive environment, encouraged by a middle-class family who valued the arts, a university that considers dance a form of research, a field of study where women far outnumber men, white skin, and a thin body in good health.[15] On the other, settler-colonial and Cartesian values that equate dance with the body and not the mind and that deem dance superficial, ornamental, or trivial also permeated my learning. As a consequence, I felt daily like a "dumb dancer" until I was in my fifties. I spent many years trying to prove to the dean of the college I attended that dance was *not* a "noncognitive activity that had no place in the college curriculum," as he referred to it, not to mention the librarian at the university where I first taught who asked me upon learning I was an assistant professor of dance for some exercises to help with slimming her thighs. The memory of that imposing building—an assertion of knowledge as a possession accessible to those who can afford it—and its librarian so plagued by normative standards of feminine beauty haunt me to this day.

I am endeavoring to use the advantages in wealth and privilege I have inherited to guide me toward being an attentive and respectful student.[16] Informed by my dumb dancer self, I also intend in these essays to analyze the ways that dance sits uncomfortably within the university—sometimes conceptualized as a way merely to relax or express feelings as an antidote to "more rigorous" academic study, and other times as a unique form of investigation and problem-solving. Additionally, I will argue for an interrogation of assumptions underlying what knowledge is. What, exactly, is it to know something and what does the assertion of knowing something imply? With Native theorizations of knowing leading the way, I hope to join in the efforts to construct more inclusive approaches to research that acknowledge the shared responsibilities of all participants engaged in understanding the world.

While I am trying to assess the kinds of access my privilege gives me, I am aware of the enormous disparities in support and prestige that the disciplines I am studying enjoy. Denigrated, decimated, or forced into assimilation, Native voices have long been ignored within the Academy or else regarded merely as subjects to be studied. The perspectives of Native scholars have only recently been accorded the degree of respect and credibility they deserve, and many universities still have not granted Native studies departmental status.[17] In contrast, the physical sciences have long held a superior position in terms of respect and funding support for research. One reading of this book could see scientific experimentation as validating Native perspectives or otherwise confirming the plausibility of their arguments. My intention, to the contrary, is to consider the different ways of describing connectedness that each offers as articulating perspectives using different descriptive systems that could inform each other. While they sometimes strongly resonate with one another, they also extend one another, posing new questions within each discipline.

Vanessa Watts (Anishinaabe and Haudenosaunee) offers a salient critique of those who are bringing aspects of Native thought into their own work but in a way that tokenizes it and fails to reckon with Native commitment to accord spirit to all beings and entities in the world. Spirit is evident in the agency that each being expresses. As she explains: "Non-human beings choose how they reside, interact and develop relationships with other non-humans. So, all elements of nature possess agency, and this agency is not limited to innate action or causal relationships."[18] Rather than refer to systems of interaction as ecosystems, she proposes that they be seen as societies, "meaning that they have ethical structures, inter-species treaties and agreements, and further their ability to interpret, understand and implement. Non-human beings are active members of society. Not only are they active, they also directly influence how humans organize themselves into that society."[19] Failure to acknowledge the full implications of this orientation toward life, as when Donna Haraway (California-based settler-scholar) refers to feminism as a form of coyote discourse without further explanation, abstracts one aspect of Native philosophy and treats it as a tool.[20] Watts similarly critiques Stacy Alaimo (Oregon-based settler-scholar) who argues that dirt may not be elevated to the status of "family member," but at least elevated to "something worthy of proper care and feeding."[21] Such a claim about dirt constructs and solidifies borders between entities that, in this case, would infer that humans' responsibility to land is analogous to an owner's duty to a pet, but land is not something that can or should be owned.

Continually contemplating Watts's critique over the course of this research, I nonetheless acknowledge that the question of whether these essays practice a form of extractivist research, in which I am cherry-picking easily available examples of Native thought without sufficiently living with their consequences, is an open one. I am profoundly grateful for the generosity of Native scholars, "word warriors" who have entered academic publishing and shared their insights and ways of conceptualizing the world.[22] Their ability and willingness to translate, while knowing that academic writing can never fully document Native knowledge, suggest a courage and commitment to sharing that I can only attempt to imagine.[23]

. . .

These are essays in the double sense of being both a scholarly genre and an effort or attempt. They are testing, endeavoring, or trying out; they are essaying. They were conceived as an archipelago and written specifically for this volume. Archipelagos emerge through erosion or, more commonly, through volcanic eruption, most often caused by tectonic plate movements. Although the islands may be very differently composed, with their land masses distributed uniquely and made of diverse amounts and kinds of earth, weathering and facing wind, rain, and tides distinctively, they remain connected under water. When formed through erosion, a once single mass slowly wears away, leaving islands whose underwater connections endure, and when volcanically formed, the islands likewise share a common or adjacent source, one that lies even further beneath the earth's crust.

Like diasporic scholar Édouard Glissant's (Martinican) vision of archipelagic thinking, this volume brings together entirely disparate fields of inquiry, and it emphasizes the process of traveling among them over any enduring product of that voyage.[24] Because its "islands" are so different from one another, it certainly aligns with Glissant's rejection of the continent as a place where one is grounded in the sense of the world as one unified large mass. It also shares with Glissant's archipelagic thought an emphasis on the rhizomatic rather than the rooted.[25] Yet where Glissant celebrates fragmentation and delves into the complexities of creolization, this volume constructs a clustered form of argumentation, with each essay connecting to the others as mutually dependent and reinforcing.

Writing about the archipelagos that comprise Oceania, Epeli Hau'ofa (Tongan and Fijian) emphasizes the process of traveling among the islands.[26] Where the colonization of the "Pacific Islands" partitioned them one from another and reduced their value to the land masses themselves, the decolonial title Oceania emphasizes the routes taken by islanders to connect to each other over millennia, transforming the region into a vast expanse traveled by inhabitants who navigate the waters to establish and renew relations.[27] Hau'ofa also asserts that a connection to the sea travels with islanders wherever they go, enabling them to make new homes in new places yet remain connected to their Oceanic identity. In a similar fashion I have made an effort to tie together the essays collected here, even as they explore different ways of describing and narrating, by centering bodily movement and its essential role in perceiving and knowing. They are fastened to one another both on the surface and underground by that movement, with the book's index serving to document ways that they overlap and draw on shared sources.

The first essay in this volume, "Walking as Place-Making," examines interconnections of memory, place, and physicality, grounding the analysis in an autoethnographic account of my own daily practice of walking in the hills and mountains of the Tongva, Chumash, and Paiute peoples, also known as the Hollywood Hills, Ojai, and the Eastern Sierra. In the last twenty years, my early-morning hill walks have taken on increasing importance as a kind of protocol through which I simultaneously immerse and locate myself in the Land.[28] As I move, I try to greet and pay respect to what is around me. *This* essay documents, in part, that process.

A vast literature on walking exists, developed within fields as diverse as anthropology, phenomenology, urban studies, geography, and sociology. What this essay adds to these discussions is a thesis about walking that integrates neurophysiological and cognitive perspectives with psychological and social experiences of walking. The essay also develops the distinction, initially observed by Michel de Certeau (unmarked), between space and place, expanding it through Charles Sepulveda's (Tongva and Acjachemen) arguments around enclosure, and connecting these to theories of colonization. Additionally, it integrates recent research on the neurophysiology of memory, arguing that memory, which is distributed throughout the body, is sometimes activated as part of apprehending the connectedness of body to place.

The second essay incorporates perspectives on processes of being, knowing, and acting ethically that have been put forth by select scholars in Native and Indigenous studies, ecological cognitive science, new materialism, and phenomenology. While these topics have been extensively studied within the disciplines of philosophy, theology, and psychology, they have rarely been examined in relation to bodily movement. In attending to the potential commonality in orientation that scholars in these fields share toward the centrality of physicality, I hope to elucidate the resonances among their articulations of what connectedness is as well as the ways their arguments constitute a rejection of Cartesian dualism.

"Embodying the Decolonial" points to the recent and enormous upsurge in the use of the adjective *embodied*, deployed in terms such as *embodied memory*, *embodied research methods*, and *embodied gender roles*. Written in sympathy with the authors' desires to emphasize the body's role in all endeavors, it nonetheless points to the way that this adjective implies its opposite—disembodied knowledge, teaching, or consciousness. Crafted to

Essaying · 9

provoke reflection on the ludicrousness of disembodied activities, it offers analyses of three terms to which the adjective has frequently been applied: *practice*, *performance*, and *scholarship*. In so doing, I would like to encourage analyses that focus more closely on what bodies actually do when they practice, perform, or conduct scholarly inquiry.

The fourth and fifth essays engage more directly with dancing, illuminated through recent developments in cognitive science and Native studies. "Remembering Dancing" looks specifically at what might be involved cognitively in recalling a dance. It considers recent neuroscientific experimentation on bodily participation in remembering that suggests that cognitive function is distributed across the entire body. It further argues that remembering is a re-creative process. At the same time, it draws on Native conceptions of the past and of memory as both social and individual. Additionally, it reflects on how this emerging theory of what memory is might prompt a reconsideration of what an archive is and how it functions.

"Dancing's Affordances" applies James J. Gibson's (unmarked) notion of affordances to the act of dancing. Gibson proposes that what organisms experience about the world is based in their assessment of their capacity to interact and engage with it. Humans do not perceive distance, weight, or grade, but rather, what is walkable, throwable, eatable, graspable, climbable, and so forth. Perceiving is not the passive registering of stimuli, but instead the active process of seeking out information, deduced through the integration of the proprioceptive sense of the body's whereabouts with the visual, aural, olfactory, and haptic sensations available. Based on this idea, the essay explores what it is that the act of dancing makes manifest and foregrounds in one's consciousness, individually and collectively. Affordances hold special pertinence for disability studies because of their potential to redefine disability as different ability, and this potential is also considered.

Because affordances have been so influential and cited as foundational for the ecological cognitive science discussed throughout this volume, this essay focuses intensively on them, asking what this theory of perception might elucidate about dancing. And because it focuses on the physical experiences of kinesthesia and proprioception as part of what perceiving is, I have also found that this way of theorizing perception has helped me imagine what many Native scholars have called "connectedness" or "relationality." Connectedness, within ecological cognitive science and, differently, for so many Native scholars, is built into and defines each moment of being in and perceiving the world.

Still, ecological cognitive scientists, even as they contest Cartesian dualism, do not align their work with a decolonial project. Native theorizations of coloniality and decoloniality therefore expand cognitive scientists' understanding of the politics embedded in their research: Neuroscience is pursuing a decolonial stance toward mind and brain insofar as it is challenging the equation between the two. These scientists need, however, to reckon with the fact that their work is also focusing on the human being in seeming isolation from all other beings and entities. How might the act of perceiving be examined as a multispecies and more-than-human process?

One of the challenges of writing these essays has been to secure connections among them while also limiting redundancies. I have tried to interlock them; however, they do not form a circle but instead resemble an arc—open ended and incomplete. The content of their form reaffirms the partiality and situatedness of knowing, but also the instability of what that even means.[29] It was particularly important for me to construct this book as an archipelago because of the many potential missteps it may be taking, chief among them insufficiently acknowledging and being respectful of Native and disability studies scholars, failing to recognize my use of white privilege, and superficially engaging with any of the disciplines discussed.

Written during a time of enormous upheavals and crises worldwide—catastrophic climate change resulting in mass extinctions and unprecedented migrations, a monumental augmentation of disparities in wealth and resources, and rising militia and gang violence, coupled with the popularity of authoritarian governments and plutocracies, these essays are intended to direct attention toward possible coalitional politics that could forge an epistemology of futurity.[30]

While the organization of these essays emphasizes the particularity of knowing, I envision that it might also suggest the potential for collective action as bodies moving, not necessarily together but rather alongside one another. Sometimes lagging behind or pushing each other out of the way, sometimes sprinting forward or in circles or curling up for a nap, I hope the essays can assist in moving us toward the portal that Arundhati Roy (South Asian) suggests opened when COVID-19 went global.[31] In that essay she argues for using the lockdown that COVID produced as an opportunity to reflect on the capitalist consumption and racial and social injustice that caused the disease. Instead of hauling massive amounts of possessions with us through the portal, she suggests we walk with only a backpack, orienting ourselves by implementing new technologies of what Simpson identifies as connection.

WALKING AS PLACE-MAKING

I could start out in one of two ways: Either I could focus on the distressed chaparral, the hubris of a vast green lawn hosting a solitary badminton net, the large swathes of cement scarring the hillside, and the abandoned plastic sacks of dog poop, or I could notice the persistence of canny plants taking advantage of leaks in a sprinkler system, the Cooper's hawks who fledged two eyases early this spring, and the newly constructed cairn with its audaciously balanced rocks. I could dwell on the greed and heedlessness that have produced the climate crisis or on the marvelous diversity of the fellow walkers I encounter each morning heading up or down the hill. Or perhaps this is a misleading choice I am giving myself.

A related fallacious choice: As I walk I could spatialize or I could emplace. I could track the coordinates of my path, count my steps, figure the distance to over there, and calculate the altitude gain. I have been taught, beginning as a small child, to practice this kind of awareness—to envision myself as a point in space that is more or less proximate to that bend in the fire road ahead or distant from the swimming pool below. I have even learned to map my full trajectory within the larger grid-like coordinates of the city at whose edges I am walking. Alternatively, I could sense the contours of the earth and my bodily adjustments to them; my connections to sage, buckwheat, and fountain grasses that line the trail; the towhees who flit in front of me in the silky, clammy humidity of morning fog; the black char left on bark from the fire five years ago alongside the newly sprouted stems after last year's meager rains. Through this porous, constantly shifting set of connections, I am "emplaced" with my surroundings.[1]

A third misleading and inaccurate dichotomy arises in the notion that I exist in the present moment as I walk and, attending to each successive moment as it unfolds, distinguish the present from being in the past or the future. In fact, my attention is often in several places and times simultaneously. Walking into a specific spot on the trail, I suddenly remember, almost as if it were happening in the present, something that occurred years earlier. Why is this? How does the engagement between the body and a particular place ignite a memory? Why and how, in the act of walking, does coming into or passing by a certain place provoke a memory of something that happened in that place, often a memory that might not otherwise be recalled? Do certain places "hold" memories, not so much as culturally designated locations set aside for the purpose of social rituals of remembering, but as individually experienced events that form part of one's past? How do the practices of spatializing and emplacing effect the act of remembering?

In what follows I will wander into some of the discussions central to theories of walking and of place-making and consider how memory, place, and physicality are interconnected, via an analysis of my own daily experience of walking. Bringing together insights from the literature on walking with Gibson's concept of affordances, I hope to integrate neurophysiological perspectives with psychological and social experiences of walking.[2] At the same time, I want to acknowledge the provisional nature of this thesis, in keeping with Native and feminist arguments that all knowledge is partial.[3]

One part of this thesis that is not provisional: I am walking on unceded Native Lands; Lands that were stolen, swindled, or coerced away from the Tongva, Chumash, and Paiute peoples.[4] These peoples, for whom the Land has served as teacher, companion, provider, and spiritual host, developed a complex and intimate relationship with these Lands, one that worked to sustain ecological balance and promote the well-being of the many other-than-human creatures living in and on it. What to do with this knowledge? I cannot repair the violent exercise in colonial domination that so radically transformed this basin, nor can I imagine my way into a Native view of the havoc it has wreaked. I cannot enter into a relationship with this Land that is in any way equivalent to the reciprocal connectivity with Land that centers Native experience. That connectivity was and is communal and continually reinforced by collective patterns of living that are unavailable to me. I can, however, attempt in my walks to honor the ancestors of these peoples, past, present, and emerging, and in so doing try to understand more deeply what that connectedness is.

Walking on Tongva Land, I know that prior to the arrival of the Spanish, the basin spreading out below me was not the "wild" and "undeveloped land" the Spanish saw, but instead, a world inhabited by over five thousand people clustered in settlements from the ocean to the San Gabriel Mountains east of Los Angeles. Studying the Kirkman-Harriman map of 1860 that depicts these settlements as well as travel routes frequently used, many of which have now become freeways, I can on a clear day locate some of them in my field of vision: to the east at least two settlements in what is now Griffith Park, to the south the coastal villages in what is now Long Beach, and to the west the sacred Kuruvungna Springs, where ceremonial dances probably took place.[5]

Since I can also sometimes see as far as Mount San Jacinto, about a hundred miles to the east, it is likely that my gaze passes over the San Gabriel Mission, seen by Father Junípero Serra to be the most successful of all the missions and for which the Tongva received a second name, Gabrielino.[6] I can also see where the Los Angeles Mission is, although it is now surrounded by multistory buildings. Despite decimating the Tongva population with the diseases they brought with them and freely raping Native women, the Spanish nonetheless succeeded in converting some to Christianity and persuading them to trade items such as baskets, pottery, deer hides, and otter pelts for glass beads, cloth, and knives.[7] Tongva also comprised the labor force for the large farming and ranching projects on the tracts of land the conquerors were awarded.[8] Because the Tongva significantly outnumbered the soldiers in the early years of colonization, efforts were made to maintain peaceful relations, although they were punished for poor work or for stealing cattle and horses.[9] However, as the Spanish population substantially increased, the 1850 Indian Indenture Act was passed, making it legal to enslave and auction off any Native people deemed to be vagrant.[10] The early twentieth century witnessed further brutality and displacement as oil was discovered. Because of the perpetual violence inflicted on them, many Tongva took refuge in Mexican communities springing up around the basin, thereby masking their identity.[11] Now, in a project of renewal and reunion, they are reuniting and establishing tribal centers.

Walking on Chumash Land in what is now called Ventura County, I can wonder whether these trails might pass by places where the Chumash gathered in preparation for their successful attack on the mission of Santa Barbara in 1824. As Tharon Weighill (Chumash) observes, they sequestered food and arms in the hills in places that only some with special knowledge knew about, and it is likely they walked this way, because the sulphureous mud they used to blacken their faces for the attack comes from nearby.[12] Af-

Walking as Place-Making · 15

ter that attack, missionaries relaxed prohibitions against ceremonial gatherings and refrained from such aggressive policing of them.

Walking on Paiute Land into the mountains of the Eastern Sierra, I know that some fellow hikers have discovered obsidian flakes and arrowheads that date back at least thirteen thousand years.[13] Paiute regularly took refuge from the valley's summer heat by traveling into these mountains. The grandeur of the mountains was commemorated through acknowledging the personhood of each boulder, slope, and peak.

Are these walks I take indulging in what Eve Tuck (Unangax̂) and K. Wayne Yang (Asian American) have identified as the "settler adoption fantasy," a way of aspiring to adopt and be adopted by the Land?[14] Am I practicing what they call "settler emplacement or replacement"—an attempt to assuage colonizer guilt and ensure settler futurity?[15] I do not think so, but there is no way to be sure. Seen primarily as land, the Lands I walk on were all stolen, and are now owned by different institutions that perpetuate settler colonialism—private land trust, city, county, and nation—while issuing an invitation to anyone who can get there to come and walk. While the land conservancy claims benevolent stewardship of the Native Land it purchased, and the National Forest Service has claimed and then set aside land for "public use," Los Angeles County has carved out parcels originally taken from the Tongva and declared them parks, probably because their steepness makes them unbuildable. I am keenly aware that I own a home within easy walking or driving distance of some of these Lands.

Body and Path

this is where the dead fox was lying
a few days later, the fox had become a skeleton moved to over there
this is where the Catalina lily comes up every June
after the fire, you could see that this whole field is full of wild peonies
the year of the big rains, this dusty trail crossed waterfalls here...
and here...and here...and here

Once able-bodied humans figure out how to do it, walking is the simplest of actions that, at the same time, could not be more complex. Substantially facilitated by the structural relationships among bones, each of a particular shape, ligaments that connect them to one another, and cartilage that cushions them, all connected by webs of fascia that weave them to the musculature, human bodies exemplify what Louise Barrett (unmarked) calls a "morphological intelligence" that enables them to walk with very little neuromuscular assistance. Indeed, robots emulating the human skeletal structure have shown the capability to walk slightly downhill without any assistance from neuromuscular effort whatsoever.[16] This might help explain the simple part of walking.

The complexity ensues from the relationing—the organizing and reorganizing of the body in relation to its surroundings—that occurs continually during walking. Following on from Gibson's work on the perceptual systems of able-bodied humans, walking involves a complex process through which the kinesthetic system, including proprioceptive, vestibular, and haptic forms of awareness of where people are, contributes vitally to their ability to assess and engage with the environment. I know where to step based on the coordinated assessment of the visual stimuli reaching the retina with vestibular information about the body's relationship to gravity along with tactile sensations of where the feet are, and changes in this information as a leg swings forward, informing my next step. This coordinated synthesizing of information that occurs across the different senses in combination with the kinesthetic awareness of how one is standing and moving, whether uphill, downhill, or on a flat surface, enables one to obtain information from the environment that, in turn, influences next actions. Humans do not passively receive input concerning their whereabouts and then actively respond to it. Instead, both perceiving and moving are continually entwined in the process of actively negotiating the environment. They are constantly in motion, no matter how minuscule the movements, and the environment is equally in motion.

Perceiving detects and calibrates the differences between an individual's motion and the motion around them, thereby determining what is more stationary and what is not. Next decisions about where and how to move are made at a subliminal level and most often not noticed. Yet perceiving becomes one of the most fundamental ways in which connectedness takes place.

Expanding on Gibson's affordance model, cognitive scientist Michael Anderson (unmarked) argues that humans do not think up an action and then execute it. Rather, they move so as to achieve a desired effect. Furthermore, they do not perceive by measuring distances or calculating angles. These measurement-oriented technologies were invented not because humans are poor at perceiving them, but because they do not perceive those elements at all.[17] They perceive throwability rather than weight, reachability rather than distance, and climbability rather than slope.[18] I have learned to assess my elevation relative to a point further up the road and thereby determine its slope, but this is irrelevant to where my foot falls next. My next step takes me both forward and up the hill. Thus, behavior is not the result of choosing the right response to a given stimulus, but instead achieving the right perceptions given the goal.

Humans begin learning how to perceive the world at birth and slowly develop the ability to integrate information from perceptual systems over time. Able-bodied infants repeat motions endlessly in order to learn that the motion of the arm may enable the hand to make contact with an object.[19] Motions of the fingers and arm may allow a young child to grasp that object and bring it to their mouth, registering its texture and taste and also the muscular strength required to support its weight. After first using stable objects to climb to standing, children then begin to coordinate the legs, balancing with the arms, to perambulate around a room, bringing them closer to people or objects, making them touchable. Eventually, they can coordinate all the senses in such a way that by looking at an object they surmise its texture, by feeling an object's weight, they know how far they can throw it, and by seeing the rockiness of a path, they know where to step.

Building on this understanding of perception, Gibson argues that what humans perceive in the world is not a stream of individual sense stimuli. Instead, our perceptual systems assess what the environment affords in terms of opportunities for engagement with it. Affordances are not strictly features of the environment; they are properties of whole situations that enable each organism to interact with its surroundings. As Gibson explains: "The simplest affordances, as food, for example, or as a predatory enemy, may well be detected without learning by the young of some animals, but in general learning is all important for this kind of perception. The child learns what things are manipulable and how they can be manipulated, what things are hurtful, what things are edible, what things can be put together with other things or put inside other things—and so on without limit." Here Gibson is listing some of the kinds of physical properties that constitute a given situation, but as becomes clear, he is also referencing social values with significant consequences. He continues: "He also learns what objects can be used as the means to obtain a goal, or to make other desirable objects, or to make people do what he wants them to do. In short, the human observer learns to detect what have been called the values or meanings of things, perceiving their distinctive features, putting them into categories and subcategories, noticing their similarities and differences and even studying them for their own sakes, apart from learning what to do about them."[20] As Gibson notes, affordances vary across species, and they also change over the course of an organism's lifetime and certainly their social situation. As people age, for example, the stream may no longer afford the possibility of jumping across it, and certain hills may no longer be climbable.

Mark Rifkin (New York–based settler-scholar) usefully adds to the categories of experience that fold into the act of perceiving affordances by considering how one might or might not feel part of "shared material circumstances that engender common sets of concrete situations and potentials for response and agency; memories and stories of such experiences that generate feelings of belonging to a group and that inform future action; histories transmitted within and across generations that offer ways of conceptually and emotionally understanding the relation between the past, present and future and the horizon toward which one moves as a member of the group, and the legacies of past actions by and toward members of the group that contour the 'field of possibility' in the current moment."[21] These cumulative kinds of connections, he argues, focusing especially on building collectivity across time, are central to Native experiences of the Land. In contrast to my mostly solitary walks, Rifkin highlights how, for many Native peoples, walking the Land is a way to collectively share long histories of involvement with it.

Each moment of walking presents a new set of affordances—avoiding a sharp rock, ducking under or skirting around foliage, clinging to the shady side of the street. In order to be respectful of the Land and all its inhabitants, choosing where to step also entails avoiding the desert stink beetle or not avoiding the puddle so that vegetation on the side of the path is not trampled and the trail gets no wider. These split-second choices are made as the relationship between body and path unfolds over time. Fitting body to path, selecting the next step, registering the consequences of that step selection, feeling the weight sinking into the foot, noting the wind brushing past the face, I fall into the rhythm of one step and then the next. In this way, all the complexity seems to feel simple and easy.[22]

Walking on flat unimpeded ground, the gaze might only occasionally focus on the path to align its direction with the body's forward motion. When walking on more complicated ground, where surfaces consist of dirt patches between exposed tree roots, perhaps alternating with flat or curved rocks of varying degrees of slipperiness, walking commands more attentiveness. Multiple perceptual systems combine to seek out the next viable step—is it possible to climb to there? To extract one's foot from here while the other foot is arriving there? To balance briefly here while passing through to there? Actively searching for routes, even on a path already defined but with multiple next-step options, perception slowly modulates to adjust and reorient to the new options. A few hours after beginning such a walk, its affordances become more and more evident. Bodily intelligence retunes itself to synchronize with the new surroundings and comes into focus as a field of possible next steps. The process of gathering information from the route reorganizes itself each time a new type of route presents itself, eventually resolving all the complexity into straightforward next steps.

Similarly, learning to ambulate using walking sticks activates whole new information-seeking processes: Where is the appropriate next site to land the stick in coordination with the foot? Will the stick's placement bear weight? If so, how much? And how much does the rest of the body need to rely on the stick's stability? Additionally, how must the body stretch, cantilever, or thrust forward to complete the step? Answers to these questions are arrived at almost instantaneously, usually, although not always, delivering a correct assessment. Learning from the successes as well as the mistakes, the walker using sticks comes to perceive the path differently. New affordances appear while others become more muted.

Focusing on this kind of malleability within the act of perceiving opens up for consideration the ways that differently abled bodies synchronize with their surroundings. People with Parkinson's, for example, may perceive a path as more cluttered or even impassable, given their assessment of their capacity to coordinate right and left legs. Walking sticks can assist, yet sometimes one's ability to mobilize left arm and right leg together may be lacking, and as a result, the affordance of foot on step and stick on higher ground does not appear.

Analyzing what has been termed *disability* from the perspective of affordances, it becomes possible to replace the hierarchical evaluation of capacities typically exercised to rate different kinds and degrees of capacity with a more heterogeneous and egalitarian understanding of each body's relationship to its surroundings. Wheelchair users, for example, can burst into motion as fast as a sprinter and turn in a tight circle far more smoothly and quickly than an able-bodied person sitting in a dining chair. The point of comparisons such as these is not to rate capacity using a single standard of measurement but rather to invite a different way of imagining the lived reality and the possible paths for all those differently abled bodies called "disabled."[23]

Walking like a Girl

are the crows learning to soar from the hawks?
tiny shoots of green grass and even some patches of moss in the
shady places after the first rains
this is where I realized I was looking at Topa Topa, seventy-five miles away
that's where the roadrunner turned around and looked at me, then headed
up the trail ahead of me, turning from time to time, to check me out

Although Gibson and Anderson both focus primarily on physical attributes of affordances for able-bodied people, it is important to note that these cannot be separated from the psychological and social properties of affordances that one acquires along with the capacity to coordinate the different perceptual systems.[24] A ball, for example, is throwable only insofar as one believes one can throw it. As Iris Marion Young (Chicago-based settler-scholar) has persuasively argued, throwing, along with many other physical actions such as standing, jumping, and running, are infused with gendered markers of identity that inform an individual's sense of who they are in the world. In advanced capitalist societies, Young explains, women (and I would further qualify here: white, heterosexual, abled-bodied women) learn ways of moving and interacting with objects that typically exhibit a more constricted use of space and greater sense of their own bodily precarity. They reach less far or throw a ball with less coordinated engagement of the entire body. They remain inhibited spatially and unintegrated physically within their own experience of a bodily wholeness and their body's relation to its surroundings. Women tend to refrain from committing fully to engagement with an affordance, moving instead in a contradictory way: "Their bodies project an aim to be enacted, but at the same time stiffen against the performance of the task.... The woman's body does carry her toward the intended aim, but often not easily and directly, but rather circuitously, with the wasted motion resulting from the effort of testing and

Walking as Place-Making · 21

reorientation, which is a frequent consequence of feminine hesitancy."[25] The hesitancy that Young describes belies a lack of confidence that folds into the actions of perceiving and acting at the same time that it reinforces one's assimilation of the identity of woman.

Similar constraints and qualifications constitute core components of other categories of identity including race, class, caste, sexual orientation, age, ability, and religious and ethnic affiliations. As Sachi Sekimoto (Asian American) and Christopher Brown (Black) observe about how race is constructed: "Race is an assemblage of sensuous realities with texture, movement, rhythm, temperature, and weight. Race materializes as a bodily, affective, and sensorial event—something that *happens*, rather than something that *is*—that involves ongoing and emergent entanglements of feeling subjects, lived sensations, symbolic interpretations, and discursive/institutional structure."[26]

It is not the case that physical affordances are apprehended that eventually become overlaid with other emotional and cultural meanings. The perception of throwability, one's psychological orientation toward throwing, and its social significance are not laminated onto the body's movement but instead thoroughly blended with it.

As Rifkin explains, and Mishuana Goeman (Seneca) further argues, for many Native peoples, Land collects the shared memories of the community. It contains the many stories that help identify complex relationships among all the entities and beings present there. In this way Land "is living and layered memory."[27] As such it may afford not only the opportunity to remember and connect with the past, but also possible courses of action in the present and future that involve how people relate to one another as well as other-than-human beings, and these ways of acting and being saturate the body and help mold its identity.

One's perception of affordances can and does evolve over time in tandem with changes in the body and one's social world. Individuals can also actively cultivate physical capacities that alter what the world affords them. However, no pre-cultural or pre-symbolic physical world exists in which left and right, ahead and behind, above and below are perceived as pure directions, separate from the many meanings each carries with it. Society itself offers affordances distributed differentially across the population.[28]

Getting to Walk and Having to Walk

> this is where the rains carved out such a gulley that the whole side
> of the hill washed out onto the road below
> this is where the two older African American gentlemen showed me
> pictures of themselves attending Barack Obama's inauguration dinner.
> we always stopped and talked politics when we met on the road
> this is where k.d. lang kissed the head of my dog

Walking is afforded to some as a form of leisure or adventure, while for others it is part of the daily labor of survival—walking to the well to procure the day's supply of water, walking to the fields, walking into town to sell what the fields yielded the day before. Nomadic life incorporates daily walking both to forage for food and to move from one site to the next.[29] Herders accompany animals in seasonal walks of transhumance.[30] For some, walking constitutes a practice of devotion, while others have endured coerced forms of walking—the chain gang and the forced marches of Indigenous peoples and of migrants. In rituals and ceremonies, walking is orchestrated into processions, pilgrimages, parades, and journeys. People take walks of exploration, walks of discovery, walks of reflection, walks of attunement. Walkers can be flaneurs or flaneuses, or Situationists practicing a derive, not to mention tightrope walkers, sleepwalkers, and dog walkers.[31] What each of these occasions for walking affords, perceptually and symbolically, is distinct, and as Rebecca Solnit (United States–based settler-scholar) has shown, varieties of walking have enjoyed very different meanings over time.[32]

The historical limits on the ability to walk are well illustrated in Sarah Jane Cervenak's (North Carolina–based settler-scholar) study of plantation slaves in the United States, whose movements were highly surveilled, limited, and controlled by their owners.[33] Like dancing and singing, walking, and more specifically wandering, signaled the unruliness of the Black body and its penchant for what was considered disorderly conduct.[34] Contemporary incarnations of this racial bias affect darker-skinned walkers, especially men, consistently, and what the darker skin affords to the lighter-skinned bystander often results in stop-and-frisk police actions as well as shootings based in the white assumption of intended violence on the part of that Black body. The knowledge that one is placing oneself in jeopardy, especially in certain regions of the country, charges what walking potentially affords a darker body with a perceptual experience that is fundamentally different from that of lighter-skinned walkers. As a Black man, choosing to take a walk is often fraught with multiple assessments of potential encounters and outcomes.

There are also many, many people whose daily routines are simply too exhausting or time-consuming to allow them to go for a walk. Others engage with a machine to construct the aerobic experience of walking. Access to wandering, rambling, wayfaring, or trekking is woven into and depends on social and class privilege. It is equally contingent on one's physical ability to walk. Disabled bodies make use of wheelchairs, walking sticks, and canes to engage in walking, and yet, some kinds of walks are unavailable to them. Undoubtedly, there are also people for whom the idea of going for a walk is aesthetically repugnant or physically repulsive.

I frame this inquiry into walking by addressing who does not or cannot walk in order to delve more deeply into who does go for a walk. Even within this relatively privileged cadre of people, many versions of a walk exist. For example, as an older woman, I am always on the lookout for certain affordances during my walk—the fine and hence very slippery overlay of grit on cement, a coyote heading up the hill, the number of other walkers scattered along the trail on whom I could call for help, the weirdly dressed or oddly behaving male walker. (I go walking too early in the morning to worry about rattlesnakes.) I have learned these affordances over the years by slipping, watching a coyote nab a small dog, and encountering various men exposing themselves. I have also experienced the same hills getting steeper as I have grown older.

As a white woman, the path does not afford me the fear that many Black men feel when sighting white police officers, or that Asian Americans feel, especially since COVID-19, largely in response to middle-aged white men. I do not groom my response to the postures of police by standing quietly, arms slightly away from the body, head tipped downward—all to appear unthreatening and unarmed, all responses to the sights and sounds of police that Black men learn from an early age.[35] The gazes of others on me do not afford me the sensation of entrapment within sets of stereotypical presumptions about who I am and how I will act, although recently a middle-aged white man patronizingly praised me for arriving at the top of a hill at my "tender young age."[36] However, I am aware that I am exercising the privilege of walking on Land that is unceded and contains histories to which I am not entitled.

What do the hills afford these other walkers, each with a different shape, size, and skin color, sporting a differently accented English, also Spanish, Persian, Mandarin, and Russian? Some glide by listening to their podcasts; others shout at their dogs while talking on the phone. Most nod cordially back at me as we pass. All of us, people and animals, leave behind footprints. These prints register a tactile interaction between ground and body; they weave the body into the Land by creating a trace, a very impermanent one, that adds its mark to all the others that have gone before it. In the summer these prints quickly blur and blend into the generally dusty texture of the path, but in the winter, after a rain, a print might remain for several days, slowly drying out yet retaining its shape until other walkers' steps cause its definition to crumble. The footprints are a reminder that the trail is shared, even if the affordances it offers vary substantially.

Place and Space

the hawk sometimes perches on the top of the transmission tower
where it has a view of the entire basin
after even the slightest drizzle the air along this part of the road
becomes pungent with the smells of eucalyptus and sage
across the canyon the rooster is crowing persistently against the background
noises of delivery vans, construction or garbage trucks, all beeping
as they back up the roads

One trail that I often walk, a dirt fire road, connects a grid of cement below to another one above. The difference between walking on dirt and cement is profound. The pavement enables carefree walking; it gives assurances regarding the flatness of the foot and uniformity of each step. It has eradicated and then glazed over anything that was there before, constructing an anesthetizing uniformity, one that encourages measuring and counting as substitute forms of interaction with the environment. The dirt trail demands attentiveness to the act of stepping because the body's weight often shifts unpredictably and things emerge that need stepping around or ducking under. It also offers much richer textures immediately adjacent: rocks, gravel, dust, many types of dried leaves and grasses cut from the surrounding hills in preparation for fire season, furrows left from rainwater surging downhill, mounds and gullies, rivulets of sandy dirt cascading off the sides of the hills. Subtly squishy, the trail bobs me along, whereas the pavement requires more bend in the knees to compensate for its rigidity.

Many scholars have noted the differences between these two experiences of walking, theorizing them as engagements with either space or place. Michel de Certeau draws attention to the difference between the grid that enforces certain routes through the city and the many instances when walkers take shortcuts, meander, or pause to observe something more closely. Place, symbolized by the grid, asserts a strategy of disciplining walkers that is frequently interrupted by tactics that walkers implement to make the city a more nuanced space.[37] Through the example of architecture, Henri Lefebvre (unmarked) similarly emphasizes the many idiosyncratic pathways through and around a given building that turn it from a place, seemingly permanent and autonomous, into a space charged through with different streams of activity that transform it into a complex nexus of mobilities.[38]

Charles Sepulveda adds crucially to this analysis of space through his consideration of containment by enclosure. Noting how the Los Angeles and Santa Ana Rivers used to flood in the spring, sometimes moistening thousands of acres of surrounding Land and thereby creating a rich ecosystem supporting plant and animal life throughout the Los Angeles basin, he also points to their now complete imprisonment within walls of cement. Entirely severed from their surroundings, the rivers no longer pose a threat to the dense residential and industrial development that has taken place along what were formerly their banks. Quoting from numerous newspaper articles that gender the rivers as female and describe their annual flooding as acts of rampage, Sepulveda demonstrates how colonization of the Land proceeded to construct the perceived necessity to tame the rivers through enclosure.[39]

Sepulveda compares this act of containment to the *monjerío*, a squalid, windowless barrack, one of the first structures to be built as part of the Spanish missions throughout California, whose purpose was the imprisonment of young girls. Taken away from their families at the age of five or six so as to estrange them from their customary ways of life, they were allowed two exits from the *monjerío* daily to attend church, and then at a suitable age, they were married off to a soldier or other official at the mission. Not only were the *monjeríos* breeding grounds for syphilis and other diseases that decimated the Native population, they also worked to remake Native conceptions of gender equality and fluidity by imposing a strict heteropatriarchal order.[40]

For Tim Ingold (Britain-based settler-scholar), boots, like roads, perform a related enclosure, cloaking the specificities of the Land, buffering the exchange between the Land's textured contours and the foot's skin and complex musculature. Not only do they support marching, they also participate in the larger colonizing project of separating the upper and lower halves of the body so as to represent mind and body respectively, with each assigned its distinct responsibilities. Feet and legs become mere vehicles for transporting the body, while the head and its extension in the hands are able to occupy themselves with cognition and complex tasks.[41] The entire body, as a sensing, feeling, and thinking organism, is itself partitioned, with each segment contributing to the redefinition of the body into a self-contained entity that moves in space. Furthering this redefinition is the primacy accorded to visual information, often colluding with systems of surveillance such as CCTV cameras and coupled with one's own internalized propensity to self-monitor actions to promote an awareness of the body as located within a grid. As if absorbing the screen's flatness, bodies become points moving through pure space.

Defining space differently, scholars such as Edward Casey (unmarked) and Paul Carter (Australia-based settler-scholar) have noted the ways that space as an abstract and mathematically oriented concept provides an epistemological foundation for the project of colonization.[42] For Casey, place is the continually emerging set of connections one has to one's surroundings, whereas space is the abstract and vacant openness onto which measurements can be affixed. To think spatially is to substitute measurement for engagement with the complexity of place and to deploy categorization as a strategy for establishing what is greater and lesser, useful and nonuseful, human and nonhuman. Conceptualized as space, land, now virginal, loses its history and becomes available to be "discovered," claimed, and conquered. Space undergirds the construction of roads, grids, boundaries, and barriers. These, in turn, create the conditions for claiming entitlement and ownership.[43] Although roads sometimes build on existing trails, adapting to the contours of the Land, just as often, they rely on maps that have already substituted for place the blank void of pure space. Seemingly installed for public convenience, roads encroach on previously established modes of transport and subsistence; they also house checkpoints and facilitate the movement of armies. As Ingold has argued, roads provide secure footing for the soldiers who have learned to march rather than walk into the territory they claim as their own.[44]

A number of Native scholars have focused on place, not only as Casey's emerging set of connections to one's surroundings but as an enduring set of attachments to one's locality, including all its inhabitants and their histories. Such attachments are cultivated and develop slowly as individuals become more familiar with the contours and histories of their surroundings. They require a taking in of whole situations that foregrounds the relations of things and beings to one another, a process that Gregory Cajete (Tewa) calls "ensoulment."[45] Establishing and reaffirming these attachments occurs in multiple ways, including visiting and telling stories about the Land as well as various ceremonial celebrations of it. Exemplary of this conception of place as contrasted with settler-colonial ideas of land, the four cardinal directions, frequently invoked in dances and other rituals, are not mere directions on a compass but also include associations with color, phases of the life cycle, seasons, mountains, and certain inhabitants of the Land, such as ceremonial plants.

At the same time, as Tuck and Yang observe, a crucial part of the history of Lands inhabited by Native peoples is their capture and transformation into property. It is because Native peoples' attachments to Land were so profoundly developed, as Cajete explains, that their forced separation from it shook the psychological and spiritual foundations of their being.[46] Place thus becomes a complex mixture of strong connection to particular localities, as well as continual awareness of and resistance to their colonized status.

As I walk in soft-soled sneakers, I cannot access the trauma suffered by the dispossessed Native peoples through whose Land I pass, but I can be mindful of it and try to maintain awareness of the mutual dependencies and complex relationships among various beings in this place. Each step affords new interactions, new possibilities. Sensing how the weight distributes across the foot, gathering information about what is near and far, listening to the screeches, caws, chirps, bulldozers, car horns, and sirens, the world composes itself; yet it is immediately recomposed as new affordances emerge. A dog gambols into the chaparral while the crow cocks its head but says nothing; the breeze shifts direction as the fog starts to recede, while a running man wheezes past, apparently secure in his knowledge that I will step to the side to afford him a straight trajectory. I am moving through and with all these events, entangled, interwoven, part of the trail, present and past. Being in this particular place is a product of these interactions rather than any boundaries that might define it.

Aspiring to take note of all these changes, I also discern how the season is changing, and with it, the plants that can endure nine months without water while others only spring to life as soon as the rains come, and still others are simply disappearing as the "Saharafication" of Southern California progresses. Deer and rabbits, hunted by the Tongva to supplement the acorns and pine nuts they gathered, are now exceedingly rare.[47] In some places the soil itself seems sandier and drier. I try to add no stress to these living beings and instead silently extend my admiration and respect. Does this matter? I hope so. Or is it just another performance of white privilege masquerading as concern? At least I am not the off-road cyclist treating the path as an outdoor gym, trampling on sage and tearing off low-hanging branches, nor will I wear earbuds to listen to a podcast or talk to a friend.[48] Instead, I aspire to be attentive to all that is around me in order to become worthy of the status of guest, or *kuuyam*, as the Tongva call it. As Sepulveda elucidates, *guest* refers to a relationship to Land and other beings that is not based in settler coloniality but rather in living sustainably, practicing tolerance for difference and respect for all beings as well as the Land itself.[49]

Remembering While Walking

>that range over there is called the Inconsolables
>after Philip passed we came here many times, repeatedly affirming
>that we were, yes, inconsolable
>two weeks ago at this time the sun was already cresting over that hill
>that's where Roksi got the gopher

As I have walked and rewalked these hills, events occur that I remember and accumulate as a kind of history of the route. These incidents become enfolded into it, adding textured densities of the past that become part of what I engage with as I walk. Who used to live there, or what the inside of that house looked like when it was being renovated; how a yard was planted, or where a scary dog lived; where a particular conversation happened, or what the Halloween decorations looked like; what the heart and peace symbol built out of small rocks looked like before a ton of earth from a post-rain carve-out up the hill covered them over. It is not that I remember all these things every time I walk, but being in a place does activate memories of its past. How is it that walking affords this recalling?

Recent research on the neurophysiology of memory has challenged the assumption that memories are representations of events that are stored in the brain. This research shows that not only are memories unstable and continually re-created, but they are also distributed across the whole body. Memories are not things, like books, that are housed on a shelf in the brain and selected for consultation. They result, instead, from complex neuromuscular patterns engaging with the environment in the moment of their re-creation.[50]

Such research suggests that when there is a sudden remembering that is provoked while passing a certain location, it is because the entire neuromusculature realigns with features in the environment similar to those occurring when the event took place. The it-happened-here-ness of memories is a product of the reactivation of sensory, neural, and muscular patterns not necessarily identical but largely similar to those from the earlier time when what is remembered occurred. A sideways glance, the curve in the road, a dampness in the air, a promontory in the distance, a wind chime, a misstep—any combination of these could facilitate the emergence of a past time. One can also remember things entirely unrelated to where one is; however, it is likely that there is some minute level of neuromuscular patterning that approximates the body's actions from that time.[51]

These memories, and even the remembering of remembering them, accumulate over the years, infusing the trail with earlier events. They imbue the now of walking with depth. Or, perhaps, they call into question the very project of dividing time into a past, present, and future, since they do not entirely feel past but instead newly re-created during *this* walk. Johannes Fabian (unmarked) has persuasively analyzed the way that the Western conception of time shifted over the course of the eighteenth century in conjunction with the new bourgeois function of travel as a project of self-discovery. Time came to be spatialized, parceled out like colonized land itself, into segments that could be measured and sequenced.[52] Thoroughly indoctrinated within this system of timekeeping, I nonetheless feel, when walking, these various pasts accompanying me in the present.

As a way to bind past, present, and future to the Land, many Native peoples use language to name places and tell stories about them. As Cajete explains, they "talk, pray, and chant the landscape into their being."[53] They narrate what happened in a particular place, thereby drawing attention to its unique features, and in this way, they pass stories along to younger generations.[54] Storytelling, as Goeman has argued, can also function as a decolonial practice in that it offers an alternative to metricized space and chronological time.[55] The act of intergenerational storytelling also serves as a technique for building collective memory. Among the Tłı̨chǫ Déné, for example, elders regularly travel with children and grandchildren to specific sites where they then tell the story of what happened there. These casual rituals bind participants simultaneously to one another and to the Land as they build a past that is shared.[56] Among the Western Apache, who practice "speaking with names," specific locales serve as synonyms for events that took place there, and simply mentioning the name of that place serves to remind the listener of that story.[57]

Eva Garroutte (Cherokee) and Kathleen Westcott (Anishinaabe and Cree) expand on these observations by noting how the vitality and liveness of stories enable them to work "co-creatively" with hearers in a process of continual re-creation. Westcott continues: "I was taught... that the story is a living being. It's not an entity in the way that, say, a bear is—because it's carried on the word. The story is able to procreate through the telling, but it is not identical with the words that people use to tell it." The living nature of stories even enables modes of interaction beyond narration: "Even at times when my purpose is not to tell the story, I may enter the story; I watch it and listen to it."[58] In this way stories function as a process of world-making.

It is also possible to view the Land as cohabitated by multiple species, each with its own narrative, as Thom van Dooren (Australia-based settler-scholar) and Deborah Bird Rose (Australia-based settler-scholar) propose.[59] These narratives, with their distinct meanings, connections, and senses of time, circulate through the canyon, crossing the trail, interweaving with one another. Each perhaps incorporates some knowledge of the others' stories as it crafts its tale of survival and coexistence. These stories are sometimes what I try to decipher as I walk, slowly accumulating knowledge about what grows where, how the water runs, where the crows klatch. They give me a deeper sense of place.

But then I trip or slip, and the world momentarily disorientates, the body unstacking and the various narratives I am trying to fathom disintegrating into unreadable fragments. It is not the case that the trail afforded a rock that I failed to notice, since affordances are constructed at the interface between what is perceived and what is given in the environment. Like my fractional comprehension of narratives populating the trail, I am afforded only a small part of what the trail contains. Slipping, often fol-

Walking as Place-Making · 31

lowed by stumbling backward, and tripping, usually prompting a lurching forward, break the rhythm of the walk, elucidating the complexity of the act of walking and the interactivity between perceptual and kinesthetic systems with their surroundings.[60]

Slipping or tripping also calls attention to the body's innards as they often experience some upheaval during the glitch. Do the gazillions of critters that compose my microbiome, at least 80 percent of the body's wholeness, also have narratives to tell each other? Are they attentive to the other species that populate the trail? Are there so many trajectories unfolding simultaneously that it is impossible to compose oneself?

The Deictics of Walking

> this particular spot always feels tranquil and serene
> the parrot's pure notes reverberate within the folds of the hills,
> making it impossible to know where it is
> after a rain the traction on the trail allows my shoes to grip
> in a way that makes walking especially dynamic

As Casey has shown, a succession of philosophers has fallen back on walking as the perfect illustration of how the body participates in place-making and how place makes the body.[61] Immanuel Kant (unmarked), whose daily walks were so uncannily regular that villagers set their clocks in reference to his passing by, established the centrality of corporeality in perceiving and organizing space based on the lived experience of up, down, back, front, and the two sides of the body.[62] He utilized walking to explain how the two sides of the body were asymmetrical and because of this, humans are able to experience the two sides of the body as distinct. Subsequently, Edmund Husserl (unmarked) used walking to emphasize kinesthesia as the binding agent that gives wholeness to the body and generates understanding of directionality and the relation between body and world.[63] Building on this thesis, Maurice Merleau-Ponty (unmarked) privileged movement more than kinesthetic sensation as the "origin" of knowing. The walking body, rather than an omniscient god or imagined pure mind, is what activates space.[64] For Merleau-Ponty, place thus becomes not a location that one occupies but a set of possible next actions. His observation "My body is wherever there is something to be done," not unlike Gibson's affordances, exists at the connection between perception and environment.[65]

Following on from Merleau-Ponty, Casey establishes here-there and near-far as the central and defining features of place.[66] In the act of walking, the relation of near to far continually morphs. Casey further dissolves the "here" half of the dyad into six aspects—above and below, in front and in back, right and left. Of these, above and below dominate based on the continuous effort of the body to retain verticality.[67] Feeling a sense of place, he argues, is produced through the continual registering of how these dyads are changing.

As appealing as this analysis is, in all its detailed elucidation of seemingly basic features of our conscious perception of the world, it is precisely the claim to being primal, fundamental, and basic that I would like to call into question. Do Casey's terms of *above-below* and so on not run the risk of establishing a level of abstraction that asserts itself as more fundamental than other more culturally specific understandings of the world? By maintaining the primacy of these categories, does Casey, and phenomenology more generally, not install a hierarchy in which the primordial experience of the unmarked subject comes first, or lies beneath, more superficial symbolic associations one's perception of space might hold? Consider the function of the *I* in this passage from Casey: "When I am getting or being placed, I perform a two-fold movement of (a) putting my body into place and *maintaining* it there; (b) undertaking specific actions *in that place*, e.g. exploring, settling in, socializing. In this way the micro-drama of holding and acting—most noticeable in activities of construction or manipulation, both of which take place close to the actor's body—is played out in more expansive scenarios of emplacement."[68] The experiences of "putting" and "maintaining" are performed by a narrator with no defining markers of identity, referring to an "actor" located in a place, both similarly unmarked. Subsequently, Casey will add that the exploring or socializing have specific histories and values attached to them. And yet, the primal and those which ornament or otherwise add to it have been established as such.

This assertion of a universal primalness is what Sara Ahmed (Pakistani British) attempts to queer in her revision of phenomenology.[69] However, why start with phenomenology in the first place if its approach necessarily derives from an unmarked position? Why build out, as Mark Rifkin does, from Merleau-Ponty's passing reference to the "historical density" of the person in order to enumerate the various conditions he considers that affect perceptions of the Land previously discussed? Why base the analysis in the reading of a static moment and then qualify it by adding that both

Walking as Place-Making · 33

the perceiver and the world are constantly in motion? Is there a way to construct a theory of perception that does not require these kinds of added qualifications or clarifications?

It could be argued that starting with Gibson's affordances performs the same split between the most basic and that which inflects it, especially without the addition of observations such as Young's concerning the centrality of markers of identity to the act of perception. Both Casey's categories of ahead-behind, up-down, and left-right and Gibson's affordances are perceiver specific, that is, dependent on the location of the perceiver for their definition. They function analogously to the grammatical category known as deictics, whose referents and meanings, according to Émile Benveniste (unmarked), are created through the act of enunciation.[70] "You," "me," "here," "there," "this," and "that," Benveniste explains, only acquire their meaning in relation to the person uttering them. Like deictics, Casey's categories and Gibson's affordances are doubly referential in that they define both the enunciator and the person (you) or place (there) that are being referenced. Casey's deictics, however, are both relative and abstract, whereas Gibson's affordances are both relative and concrete. The ahead and behind are neutral, intangible hypotheticals, whereas the rock, pavement, and branch, as well as the barking dog and speeding cyclist, are specific and material.

Why does this matter? The claims for a universal baseline or foundation to the act of perception provide the rationale for more general claims to the universality, omniscience, and potential for objectivity in knowledge-making. Affordances, in contrast, ground a conception of knowledge as always limited and qualified. The two approaches also entail strongly contrasting theories of how places are constructed. Casey posits that place-making follows from the ongoing reckoning with what is ahead and behind, such that people first "hold"—that is, settle in—and then "act," as in engage with their surroundings. Through these sustained engagements, humans come to know a place and be emplaced in it. In this way, meaning accretes, layering onto the blankness of ahead and behind. Casey thus spatializes before becoming emplaced, and this erases not only the specificity of the actions but also the history of contact between the body and its surroundings.

Affordances, sensed with the entire body and synthesized kinesthetically, come with inbuilt memories from which histories can be constructed. They help define who the person is and how they might come to know and engage with their surroundings. They make possible the act of remembering within the palpable flux of the world. They adhere body with surroundings, not in the way that a substance like glue fixes one thing to another, but as actions, produced through a continual moving, bind two fluxes—that of the body and that of its surroundings—together. Perhaps a better metaphor is that of weaving together, which has the advantage of leaving a trace, like the thread that is being woven, of the path the body has taken. Regardless of the metaphor used, the body is, most crucially, an interface in which perception is an act of connection.

Pausing

> "how come I never noticed you before," I say to the cactus whose blooms are slowly transforming into the pears that give the cactus its name

Wambling along through the writing of this essay, I have endeavored to illustrate how affordances define my daily walks and offer me a moving sense of place. Bypassing a phenomenological understanding of place, I have tried to emphasize my partial and sometimes fragmented experience. The walk this writing has taken, more a meander than a straight line, also explored how body and site catalyze memory, saturating some sites with connections to a past. It rambled up fire roads and barely legible paths as well as strolled along streets lined with fancy houses and apartment buildings, each chock full of stories.

Walking can serve as a practice of place-making, establishing knowledge while in motion, knowing while and through moving. But is it any different from the way humans come to know in doing any activity? Or, put differently, could analogous inquiries not be conducted into sitting-reading, standing-cooking, moving-dancing, or riding a bicycle?

BEING, KNOWING, AND ACTING

Then the light shed down sharply golden and I began to think. Thinking saved me. Perception saved me. I saw that the spiders were just substance. Not bad, not good. We were all made of the same stuff. I saw how we spurted out of creation in different shapes. How for a time I would inhabit this shape but then I'd be the lace on my sister's shoe that had dropped off her foot onto the weeds and tamped grass, or I'd be the blue pot my parents argued about, or maybe something else. There was nothing but the endless manufacture of things out of nothing. I saw the changing and exchanging of shapes. The grass growing all around me, now, would one day be the cow, the milk, the flesh of the calf, then me. —LOUISE ERDRICH (Chippewa), *The Painted Drum* (2005)

Vine Deloria Jr. (Standing Rock Sioux) describes it as "the continuing creation of reality," an attuning to the flux of both self and world. Brian Burkhart (Cherokee) calls it "our locality," or the kinship, built from the ground up, in which all beings are immersed. Vanessa Watts names it "Place-Thought" as a way of describing the interconnectedness of sensing and knowing. Karen Barad (California-based settler-scholar) identifies it as "intra-action" or "intra-active entanglement." Edward Casey calls it "implacement," or the indissoluble continuity between body and its surroundings. Margrit Shildrick (unmarked) invents the term *concorporeality*, the state in which we live—continually striving to maintain borders and boundaries between self and other. Merleau-Ponty names it "flesh," the condition of "not matter nor mind, nor substance, but an elemental medium—like air or fire—in which self and world are constituted in mutual relation."[1] James Gibson and Anthony Chemero (unmarked) describe it as "affordances," otherwise known as the content of our experiences.

These authors' inquiries are centered in radically disparate fields of inquiry—Indigenous and Native studies, new materialism, phenomenology, and cognitive science—that address entirely distinctive realms of life: the values and meanings central to Native identity, the relations between different types of matter, the lived experience of being in the world, and the functioning of perception and cognition. Even to refer to Native studies or cognitive science, however, as a chorus of voices that are singing in unison is misrepresentative. These fields are populated by diverse scholars who often dispute and critique one another.

And yet, all these authors, each in a very particular way, agree on the constant changingness of the lived world and the continual creation and re-creation of a lived reality even as their investigations focus on entirely different arenas of experience and methods of inquiry. Deloria's, Burkhart's, and Watts's articulations of Native philosophies emphasize how the world is shared by all beings, both animate and inanimate, that are residing in it. They found their inquiries in the assumption of a fundamental kinship among all beings. Barad's new materialism, in contrast, bases its claims in the physics of molecular matter. The phenomenological approach articulated by Casey, Shildrick, and Merleau-Ponty focuses on introspective investigation of how and what one perceives. Gibson's and Chemero's theories of perception derives from studies of visual perception conducted on people moving through the world.

All these authors actively dismiss the conception of a split between subject and object, and instead are searching for a way to articulate a fundamental oneness out of which divisions, separations, and differences continually emerge. Further, their projects, while sometimes emphasizing the metaphor of connection, are not about showing how things that are separated become connected. Rather, their projects illuminate just how entwined humans are with the world, so much so that the perception of a stable autonomy must continually be renewed and reinforced. Their projects also strongly contest assumptions about the human as the pinnacle of evolutionary achievement, while also asserting the partiality of the observer's knowledge.

Taken together, might these distinct projects intimate a larger epistemic shift, one that is slowly undoing fundamental assumptions about knowledge production that have prevailed in the West for the last four hundred years? I hope so, since the urgency of these inquiries becomes even more evident in the face of what coloniality, unregulated capitalism, and sciences based in extractivism have produced: a failing biosphere, food insecurity, exceptional disparities in wealth and resources, and increased state and militia violence. In what follows I want to emphasize how these diverse inquiries could guide a reimagining of humans' status within the world based more in equity and reciprocity. In so doing, I will take up three areas of resonance among them: conceptions of being and of knowing and their ethical consequences.[2] All three—being, knowing, and acting ethically—are the product of bodily movements, however minimal or slight, and it is these movements that establish repeatedly a sense of connection with and distinctiveness from all other entities and beings in the world.

Before taking up this inquiry, however, I want briefly to reflect on the act of summoning these voices onto the page together and how this is being done. First of all, while I frequently summarize their arguments, I feel a strong need continually to identify who is arguing what and to keep their voices prominent as a way of paying respect to them. My voice resides in the summaries of their arguments, some of which I will undoubtedly fail to present adequately, and also in the sequencing of their voices and the observations about the centrality of movement in their arguments.[3]

But in what senses do my assertions of resonance among these authors perform a masking over, a denial, a violence even, of their differing heritages and circumstances? How might they feel about finding themselves here on these pages together? In what senses am I willfully ignoring the particularities of how and why their arguments are being made? At this point are these scholars pivoting abruptly and walking away? Shrugging their shoulders? Peering over their reading glasses? Even as I can't decipher what these bodies are doing, it is certainly necessary to ask these questions.

being/moving

A strong theme running through the work of several Indigenous and Native studies scholars focuses on connecting humans to the larger universe of beings, both animate and inanimate, and continually affirming the fact of relationships among all beings. They argue that consciousness should be seen as suffused throughout the known world. George "Tink" Tinker (Osage), for example, discusses rocks as nonhuman entities that are understood as having consciousness within Indigenous systems of knowledge.[4] Rocks and rivers join insects, plants, and all animals in their understanding of a purpose to their being. Because all beings in the world are both "alive and thinking," as Watts explains, they pursue choices about where and how to interact with other beings. These relationships form complex webs of mutual engagement, sometimes conceptualized in Western science as niches, habitats, or ecosystems, and yet the depth of these relationships has yet to be fully comprehended because, as Watts identifies, the agency exerted by all things on one another can take many forms.

Burkhart names this experience of reciprocal relationships one's "locality." Locality is a way of referencing the interface between self and the surrounding Land, in which Land signifies the actual physical substance of what is around people as well as the history of their connections to it. It also refers to the way that any given thing consists of a multiplicity of meanings, histories, and values.[5] Locality builds from one's physical presence as it articulates and enacts the relations to all that surrounds it. Locality is a process that is literally built step by step. It is also a process that does not depend on a stable or enduring ground. As Laura Harjo (Mvskoke) explains, developing her analysis by centering her writing in the history of her tribal affiliation as Mvskoke and the forced displacement of these people in the early nineteenth century, locality instantiates diversely in concrete, ephemeral, metaphysical, or even virtual forms.[6] She points to the capacity of Native peoples to continually remake connections to their changing circumstances in order to affirm and create community.

Evidence of these reciprocal relationships, Brendan Hokowhitu (Māori, Ngāti Pūkenga) asserts, can be found through attending to the immediacy of everyday experience.[7] For him both selfhood and knowledge are produced through this engagement with the immediate. In noticing the small, seemingly incidental, encounters in which one participates throughout the day, it becomes possible to tap into an awareness that, as Erdrich describes at the beginning of this essay, "We [are] all made of the same stuff." Thus, as I understand it, the rock's consciousness changes as it tumbles down the hill, settles in place, and resists and succumbs to wind, rain, and surrounding vegetation, with the verbs I have chosen to describe its varieties of action attempts to document the particular moments of how its being continually emerges. Its tumbling, settling, and resisting are both actions and forms of knowing. Similarly, human selfhood transforms as bodily action generates new interactions in each moment.

Developing out of their training in theoretical and particle physics, Karen Barad also emphasizes the fundamental connectedness of all matter, affirming an entanglement among all beings.[8] For Barad the primary ontological units are not "things," but phenomena defined as "the ontological inseparability of agentially intra-acting 'components.'"[9] With the use of the term *phenomena*, Barad emphasizes the processual nature of being; matter is constantly shifting, changing, and remaking itself. By coining the term *intra-acting*, Barad calls into question the assumption that events take place between separate entities, and instead emphasizes that different forms of matter are continually producing themselves as distinctive through their ongoing engagement with one another. This ongoing coming into uniqueness constructs what Barad calls a "cut," a separation within entangled matter that, unlike the object-subject split, identifies difference as momentary and continually renegotiated.[10]

Could this be an argument at the atomic level for what Tinker and Watts are describing as how all things form relations with one another? It seems less focused on the mutually supportive and interdependent qualities of what Watts describes as societies, but it does emphasize the processual nature of being's emergence. As Barad explains: "All bodies, not merely 'human' bodies, come to matter through the world's iterative intra-activity—its performativity. This is true not only of the surface or contours of the body but also of the body in the fullness of its physicality, including the very 'atoms' of its being. Bodies are not objects with inherent boundaries and properties; they are material-discursive phenomena. 'Human' bodies are not inherently different from 'nonhuman' ones. What constitutes the 'human' (and the 'nonhuman') is not a fixed or pregiven notion, but nor is it a free-floating ideality."[11] As material-discursive phenomena, the distinctiveness of all beings in the world continually emerges even as the connectedness of all beings endures. Watts also addresses the rock's agency as something that endlessly emerges, and she rejects any special status for the "human." She also emphasizes the obligation of all beings to one another. If Watts and Barad are partially aligned in this, I want to underscore that it is through matter in motion that their senses of being are constructed.

Casey and Shildrick likewise emphasize the fundamental connectedness of things, stressing the ongoing struggle of establishing separations between self and world. Casey focuses on the in-flux-ness of one's sense of self and surroundings. His notion of implacement defies stable positioning, instead emphasizing how perceptions of self and world are in continual transformation. Shildrick adds to this the argument that much of what Michel Foucault (unmarked) calls "discipline" derives from the imperative to construct the self as an autonomous entity when, in fact, personhood is far more porous.¹² The distances people maintain between one another, the direction and quality of their focus, their manner of greeting, bodily posture, the speed and force of any gesture—these are all habits of moving that are learned, but they also continually define who a person is. Such movements help construct isolable individuals and the social relations in which they are enmeshed.

In conducting their phenomenological examination of experience, Casey and Shildrick also draw on observations about the body made by Merleau-Ponty. *Flesh*, the term he uses to refer to the mutually constitutive relations between self and world, emphasizes both the bodiliness and continually changing nature of experience.¹³ As Casey explains, Merleau-Ponty emphasizes movement as the "origin" of knowing. The moving body, rather than an omniscient god or imagined pure mind, is what activates space.¹⁴ Place thus becomes not a location that one occupies but a set of possible next actions. For Merleau-Ponty: "What counts for the orientation of the spectacle [around me] is not my body as it in fact is, as a thing in objective space, but as a system of possible actions, a virtual body with its phenomenal 'place' defined by its task and situation."¹⁵ Here Merleau-Ponty emphasizes both the intra-active nature of physicality and the mutual *entanglement*, to use Barad's term, of self and world.

Merleau-Ponty's description of bodily capacities parallels the work of Gibson and his concept of "affordances" as an interface between the organism and its environment that constitutes its lived reality. Like Merleau-Ponty's notion of flesh, affordances do not abide in either the individual organism or its surroundings. Instead, they manifest as the product of the motions of both the individual entity and its world. As Gibson explains:

> If a terrestrial surface is nearly horizontal (instead of slanted), nearly flat (instead of convex or concave), and sufficiently extended (relative to the size of the animal) and if its substance is rigid (relative to the weight of the animal), then the surface affords support. It is a surface of support, and we call it a substratum, ground, or floor. It is stand-on-able, permitting an upright posture for quadrupeds and bipeds. It is therefore walk-on-able and run-over-able. It is not sink-into-able like a surface of water or a swamp, that is, not for heavy terrestrial animals. Support for water bugs is different.... Terrestrial surfaces, of course, are also climb-on-able or fall-off-able or get-underneath-able or bump-into-able relative to the animal.¹⁶

Gibson notes that affordances vary across species and they also change over the course of an organism's lifetime. Thus, different species and organisms dwell in particular environments, or what Gibson calls "niches," thereby composing webs of overlapping worlds of potentialities. The local moment of coming into separateness from the environment, what Barad calls the "cut," is the moment of perceiving the affordance.

In perceiving affordances, an organism activates an awareness of the world and of itself. It notices a relation between a capacity that it has and a feature or features within the environment. Yet, as Chemero explains, humans seldom perceive affordances themselves. Instead, they perceive a lived reality. Experiments measuring peoples' estimations of a ball's weight, for example, found that it was judged heavier if subjects thought it was to be thrown than if they were told to walk it to the target. Similarly, if they had been tired out by first walking on a treadmill, they perceived the distance to a target as further away if they thought they would be walking a ball to the target versus throwing the ball at the target.[17] What these kinds of experiments show is how the perceived world is always a product of the ongoing registering of bodily capacity relative to its surroundings.

Affordances exist even if no specific organism is there at that moment to engage in them, because they endure as a theoretical possibility that the organism could enact. At the same time, the affordance is not a property of the environment. Because of this, the concept of affordances does not imply the existence of entirely separate realities for each organism. All members of a given species share a world, although that world can be modified according to age, ability, and to some degree, experience.

Gibson's theory of affordances extends to include the social capacities of humans and the multiple ways in which they engage with each other.[18] Because of this it seems plausible to imagine that affordances could serve as a grounding concept for theories of cultural consistency and continuity such as Pierre Bourdieu's (unmarked) habitus. Equally, as discussed in the preceding essay, affordances might align with more phenomenologically oriented inquiries such as Young's observations about women in advanced capitalist societies as experiencing a more inhibited sense of space, a more fragile bodily capacity, and a discontinuous sense of bodily movement.[19] Young's example of "throwing like a girl" could be read as the routinization of perceptual activity that identifies the ball as less throwable for women. The experience of femaleness within a patriarchal and sexist society influences the perception of throwability and, in turn, the ball's throwability contributes to the experience of femininity.

Unlike Barad, who focuses on particle-level physics, Gibson dwells in the environment that humans can sense and perceive, yet like the new materialist thesis, he argues strongly for the inseparability of an organism from its environment. Affordances also recall Watts's notion of "Place-Thought," which she defines as "the non-distinctive space where place and thought were never separated because they never could or can be separated. Place-Thought is based upon the premise that Land is alive and thinking and that humans and non-humans derive agency through the extensions of these thoughts."[20] Gibson would probably not ascribe thought to a set of stairs or a ball, and yet the theory of affordances does animate them insofar as they become climbable or throwable and thus are collaboratively connected to those species capable of engaging with them. Watts's "Place-Thought," however, ascribes such capacities for thinking to all beings in the world, and it stresses the process of mutual discovery.

When I consider these scholars together, it seems that they are endeavoring to elucidate, albeit using very different frameworks of analysis, an intrinsic connectedness between body and world in which the sense of being is produced through bodily actions that reveal ongoing yet changing relations to surroundings with variously textured histories. Walking, running, twisting, and falling yield very specific senses of being, as do blinking, standing still, or reading a book. Each action opens up particular perceptions of the world and all it contains. In this way of conceptualizing being, the body is not an object, nor is it "told" by the mind what to do. Rather, the step itself is intelligent and its engagement with the path is a thought. My connectedness takes place through the perception of next possible actions, as determined by social norms and prescriptions for behavior as well as rocks and plants. Although the way that movement produces being is most often not registered consciously, it is possible to attend to it and thereby experience, as Watts notes, "the non-distinctive space where place and thought were never separated."

Still, this experience of being can be acknowledged more easily in some contexts than others. Especially within Western and settler-colonial socialities, the desire for stability and the need to experience an autonomous and reliable sense of self that is separate from its surroundings beckons powerfully. The emphasis on individual achievement, mastery, and wealth acquisition and retention all work to obscure flux, replacing it with numerical measurements of time and space, against which the solid and steady individual can be compared. The Native community portrayed in Simpson's essay enables a different experience of being to emerge more easily, one that attunes to flux and the porousness of both body and surroundings. When mutual support rather than competition is the goal, the experience of being as motion filled becomes more accessible. In calling attention to this, might these scholars, all of whose arguments carry with them entirely specific motivations, circumstances, and histories, not walk away but remain, albeit reluctantly, in the vicinity?

knowing/moving

The acquisitiveness of settler-colonial epistemology drives conceptions of knowledge toward a fact-based understanding of what knowing is. Knowledge becomes the collection of truths that have been discovered, verified, and repeatedly proven, and knowing consists in the assimilation and memorization of these facts. Knowing consists of arriving at certainty and holding on to that truth. Libraries and archives serve to store these truths and facts, organizing them according to subject and imbuing them with an illusory permanence. Smartphones and Google facilitate this practice of acquiring knowledge through providing easy access to definitions, histories, directions, dates, times, and places. Fitbits translate somatic experiences into numbers of steps taken, heart rate, and other metrics deemed important as measurements of good health. In converting these experiences into numbers, they seem also to downplay and even devalue actual physical experience in favor of the hard, cold facts. Habits form around consulting the internet and the momentary ingestion of information it provides, confirming knowledge as the verbal expression of bite-size renditions of what the world is and how it works.

Native conceptions of knowing, as I understand them, offer a starkly contrasting orientation. Knowledge may revolve around truths, but any and all such truths are relative and mutually determined in the moment of their consideration. Land and locality hold truth, yet it is mutable and open to reinterpretation. Knowing is a journey that never ceases.[21] The world is composed not of things but of relationships.[22] Rather than acquired, knowledge is shared, and furthermore, it should be used for the common good of all. Action, whether it results in speaking, dancing, cooking, walking, swimming, or sitting quietly (of course, this list is much, much longer), is what yields knowledge.

Reflecting on this epistemological orientation, I return to Simpson's assertion that knowledge develops most especially through patient observation and quiet attentiveness.[23] Devising contact that is respectful of all life and then sharing this bond with trusted others is a process of building knowledge in ways that mutually benefit everyone. For Simpson, Land, crucially, functions as vital teacher, guide, provider, and companion: "Coming to know is the pursuit of whole body intelligence practiced in the context of freedom, and when realized collectively it generates generations of loving, creative, innovative, self-determining, inter-dependent and self-regulating community minded individuals."[24] As Simpson details, "whole body intelligence" is galvanized in an Indigenous approach to world-making that focuses on alignment with rather than domination over, and it promotes a willingness to decenter human superiority.[25] It also encourages a constant repositioning of oneself as a learner, validating bodily experience as a reservoir of knowledge. The "whole body" participates.

With his notion of locality, Burkhart locates "whole-bodied-ness" at the interface between self and the surrounding Land, in which Land signifies the actual physical substance of what is around one as well as the history of one's connections to it. It also refers to the ways that any given thing consists of a multiplicity of meanings, histories, and values. "Things display their nature in our experiences as a continual unfolding of their being,"[26] he explains, as part of one's continuing development of kinship with and in the world. A thing's expression of multiplicity is not something external to it, as a representation or symbol might be, but instead is an intrinsic part of their being in relation.[27] Further, all kinship relations are in constant motion, and this already being in motion constitutes the most fundamental aspect of life itself.[28]

Gibson, it seems to me, concurs about the motion entailed in knowing, yet he frames his argument through the process of perceiving. For him, affordances provide the content of experience, and this, simply, is what is known. Perception entails the active seeking out of information and the equally active assessment of that information in relation to the perceiver's bodily status. The awareness of perceived information is distributed across the entire body. Knowing is an extension of perceiving.[29] Children, through their combined sensory systems, come to learn more and more about the world. They are also made aware of their surroundings through the pictures they are shown, the books they learn to read, and the stories they are told. However, these, in and of themselves, are not knowledge. Books simply facilitate knowing by giving their readers the opportunity to imagine and consider different experiences of the world.

Gibson considers perception not only as active but also as meaning filled, thereby rejecting the notion that meaning is ascribed to events after they have been perceived. Traditional Western notions of knowledge presume that sensation occurs prior to interpretation and understanding, whereas Gibson's thesis fuses them into a single operation. Knowledge builds from birth as one perceives more and more about the world, incorporating organism-specific experiences along with the general capacities of the species to engage with the world.[30]

Barad likewise emphasizes the specificity of the relationship between what is known and how it becomes known, basing much of their argument on Werner Heisenberg's and Niels Bohr's (both unmarked) conclusions that the system of detection used to investigate things influences the outcome. Heisenberg's indeterminacy principle derives from his attempts to measure light using different instruments, with the result that light appears in one set of experiments to consist of particles and in another set to appear as waves. Barad develops the notion of intra-action from this, arguing that there are no fundamental particles or entities from which all things are constructed. Rather, the apparatuses used to measure things are always historically contingent and only locally meaningful. The fact that light can appear to be a particle or a wave is the product of the intra-action between the measuring apparatus and light. Parallel to Burkhart's conception of "things" as constantly unfolding and changing in their significance, Barad proposes that knowing is not exclusive to humans because it entails "part of the world making itself intelligible to another part.... We do not obtain knowledge by standing outside of the world; we know because 'we' are *of* the world."[31] Knowing is the product of being and moving in the world, and it is illusory to imagine that any form of inquiry, whether machine or human, stands apart and separate from complete immersion in the world.[32]

Deloria has long called for science to consider Native views of the constitutive relations of humans with nonhuman species, ecological systems, natural processes, and all aspects of Land. "We are all relatives," he argues, should be used as a methodological tool.[33] Rather than approaching each species as isolable and distinct, Deloria attends to their symbiotic and interdependent relationships. By tracing out these webs of interrelationships, knowledge as isolable facts evaporates, and the dynamism that defines connections becomes apparent.

Trained in both Western and Native approaches to botany, Robin Wall Kimmerer (Potawatomi) similarly focuses on kinship. She distinguishes doing science from a scientific worldview that reinforces a false sense of control and even dominance over the world, leading to a distancing of the acquisition of knowledge from the responsibilities that accompany it. Instead of this scientific worldview, she argues that doing science enables a profound intimacy with the world in all its mystery, so much so that many scientists often find it a deeply spiritual pursuit. Furthermore, she explains, to engage in scientific inquiry from an Indigenous point of view is to assume that

> humans have much to learn from other species and are viewed as somewhat lesser beings in the democracy of species. We are referred to as the younger brothers of Creation, so like younger brothers we must learn from our elders. Plants were here first and have had a long time to figure things out. They live both above and below ground and hold the earth in place. Plants know how to make food from light and water. Not only do they feed themselves, but they make enough to sustain the lives of all the rest of us. Plants are providers for the rest of the community and exemplify the virtue of generosity, always offering food. What if Western scientists saw plants as their teachers rather than their subjects? What if they told stories with that lens?[34]

Reaffirming Deloria's claim that we are all relatives, Kimmerer repositions the scientist as a student engaging in respectful relations with all beings.

Kimmerer might say that the plants also study us, since, as she explains, their propagation is often dependent on our mobility and also our habits of selective harvesting that preserve their robustness. As Barad also observes, some forms of matter study other forms, and this kind of inquiring could be undertaken variably across many if not all beings. From this understanding of the intraconnectivity of all things, knowing as a practice of relationing becomes the act of affirming this intraconnectivity. Knowing is, in part, the experience of the mingledness of all things.

As a continual collaborative process, knowing does not take place apart from one's engagement with the book, the machine, or the plant. Knowledge does not exist on its own, nor is it objectively proven and permanent. The act of knowing is just that, ongoing bodily actions—a tilting of the head to one side, a shift of weight, an exhalation, a turning away or tensing toward or pushing against—that yield perceptions that reveal what can be known in any given moment.

Returning to Simpson's example of the young girl observing the squirrel, I imagine how the practice of patience physicalizes as both a quietness that inhibits abrupt motion and an expansion of attentiveness that, in turn, attunes the body to a larger and more detailed world. Stilling certain kinds of motion, such as large movements of the limbs, can throw awareness onto the tiniest of movements that precipitate new apprehensions of others' movements nearby. As I will discuss in the coming pages, stillness could also function as a precursor to a fixedness and fortification of the body's borders that allows a sense of isolated autonomy and even superiority over one's surroundings. However, patience, as Simpson details it, is not simply about enduring and certainly not about separating oneself from surroundings. Practicing patience entails reinvigorating an active alertness and calm energizing of attentiveness so that what is unfolding becomes increasingly evident. It invites renewal and an increasingly porous state of being. Patience is thus a combination of movements that continually kindle the curiosity that invites knowing.

Patience, for Simpson, also serves to facilitate respectful relations, allowing the in-motion observer to honor what is being observed. The mandate to accord respect is central to Native epistemology, and I want to mark this difference from Western approaches that emphasize "objectivity," since it is, perhaps, a core difference that could prompt bodies on these pages to walk away. Where Western science has traditionally attempted to cleanse its investigations of all affect and attitude, it is my understanding that Native conceptions of being and knowing are inextricably linked to ethical action.

acting/ethically

Following on from an understanding of the fundamental conjoining of all things and the awareness that knowledge derives from engagement with that connectedness, Deloria considers which actions matter and which do not. He argues that "in the moral universe all activities, events, and entities are related, and consequently it does not matter what kind of existence an entity enjoys, for the responsibility is always there for it to participate in the continuing creation of reality."[35] Because there exists a reciprocity among all entities and beings, each enables the others to intervene in the world's becoming.[36] This includes the many spirits, ancestors of the currently present and other enduring presences, that dwell at specific sites or migrate from place to place. All these entities should be embraced and allowed to participate in the fact of their connectedness with all other entities.[37] This reciprocity is what settler colonization violated so aggressively and violently.

Yet for Burkhart, the project of settler colonization can never be complete because it cannot reckon with or capture the fundamental connectedness to locality maintained by Native peoples. The annihilation, enslavement, and coerced assimilation forced on Native peoples failed to completely eradicate their sense of connection to place: "Just as our being in its locality resists colonization—a remainder of our being always exists in the land in contrast to the coloniality of our being as colonized people—so the being of the land itself resists colonization. A remainder of the being of the land as locality always exists in contrast to the coloniality of land itself as a de-localized abstraction, as mere land. The colonization of our subjectivity and of land is never complete. Neither can be fully colonized because of their locality."[38] Because colonization does not acknowledge, much less value, the multiplicity of beings in the world, and instead privileges humans as exceptional and more advanced than all others, it reduces place to mere space. Such a reduction, however, can never be completed.

In order to understand better what Deloria and Burkhart are arguing about ethical action, I want to consider in more detail what colonization introduced and accomplished. As many decolonial theorists have argued, colonization's presumed superiority of humans over the rest of the natural world was also grounded in the presumed superiority of some people over others. Central to the colonial undertaking, according to Enrique Dussel, is the formation of the ego conquiro, or self that conceives of the capacity to claim superiority and exert control over another. Expanding on this thesis, Ramón Grosfoguel argues that the colonial project emerged in the wake of what he calls the "four epistemicides," or systematic destruction of worldviews. This was accomplished through the expulsion of Jews and Arabs from Spain and the burning of their libraries, the Inquisition's extermination of women and the knowledge held in their bodies, and the "discovery" and conquest of the Americas. The first three of these secured a Christian patriarchal base for Spain from which the conquering armies

Being, Knowing, and Acting · 49

brought Christianity to the New World as rationale for plundering its many and varied resources. France and England soon followed Spain and Portugal in carving up and claiming large swathes of North and South America as well as Africa.

For Sylvia Wynter, the Spanish and Portuguese explorers of West Africa in the 1440s inaugurated the first and defining moments of colonization, when they adopted the slavery already being practiced. As those explorers implemented it, transatlantic slavery entailed a necessary calculation of the degree of humanness of various African peoples based on observations of their daily habits and practices as well as verbal exchanges about their belief systems. Like the Indigenous peoples they would soon encounter in the Caribbean and Americas, Africans were variously seen by Europeans to be savages or subhuman, having a soul and hence capable of Christian salvation, or existing as beasts who were unable to be incorporated into the Christian world. In either case the conquistadors established what they deemed to be rational grounds for capture and enslavement, subjugation, or extermination.

Dussel argues that the ego conquiro underlying colonization paved the way for the ego cogito, the Cartesian separation of mind from body that subtended scientific inquiry and the distinction between the subjective and the objective.[39] Wynter sees the two as inseparable and mutually enabling. The ego cogito designated a privileged arena for mental functions seen as separate and independent from bodily influences and needs. This ego harbored the rational processes of logic, language, and reasoning, in contrast to the demands for pleasure and sustenance made by the body. Together the ego conquiro and the ego cogito made possible the claiming and apportionment of land, the displacement and subjugation of peoples, and the extraction of multiple forms of wealth, including minerals, animals, and plants, all actions that ruptured communities and ecosystems.

As part of the emergence of the egos conquiro and cogito and the new episteme that they made possible, certain technologies were introduced that helped consolidate this new way of thinking about and knowing the world. As previously discussed, Ingold points, in particular, to boots and chairs, items that appeared during this historical period and that facilitated the formation of a newly autonomous, empowered self.[40] Boots walled the feet off from the land, their stiff soles and sturdy sides numbing the foot and depriving it of its capacity to obtain information, as Gibson would say, from the soil, rocks, and plants. They transformed the feet into mere machines of transport, tacitly giving even greater privilege to the eyes and the head. Complementary to this, chairs invited a more static positioning of the body, certainly stilling it more than when standing, and thus constructing an opportunity to identify the head as the source of knowledge. When converted into wagons, carriages, and other forms of transport, chairs lifted the body up, giving it the illusion of separation from and superiority over others. Although two among many other technologies that facilitated colonization, these examples are important to consider as valuable factors in the success of the colonial project because they directly address the role of bodily connection to surroundings.

To the egos conquiro and cogito, Burkhart adds a third, the ego constituo, that references the act of planting crops.[41] Settler colonists first moved onto the land as if it were uninhabited and then worked the land to yield sustenance for themselves while dismissing the fact that Native peoples had practiced agriculture for centuries. Following John Locke's (unmarked) argument that contributing one's labor to the alteration and improvement of something enables ownership of it, they took possession of the land and then claimed the right to pass it along to their heirs.[42]

Burkhart, Watts, and many other Native scholars would call out the absurdity of claiming ownership over Land, and they decry the violence issuing from such claims. Deloria's moral universe is based in entirely different epistemological tenants that feature reciprocity and mutual acknowledgment. The improvements to the land claimed by settler colonists were violations of the various beings who had thrived there successfully for generations. And the marshaling of bodily action to justify ownership desecrates both body and Land.

In this critique of settler colonialism and the body's role in its success, I find potential alignment with other scholars gathered on these pages. Gibson, for example, expresses skepticism about fundamental aspects of the ego cogito by contesting the categories of space and time as measurable categories of experience. He also points out that Locke's assertion about "form, size, position, solidity, duration, and motion" as qualities inherent within an object that are distinct from what we perceive about it is completely irrelevant and useless.[43] Further, he argues that we do not perceive geometric space or chronological time—both constructs that facilitate coloniality because of the ways they parse the lived world and thereby make it available for ownership.

Gibson's research includes a strong rejection of traditional experimentation with vision in which subjects were required to remain seated with the head fixed to a bite bar and one eye covered in order to measure the responses of the open eye to various stimuli. Such experiments derive from and then confirm the assumption that the eye's retina functions like a camera taking a snapshot. Underlying this assumption is an analogy between the body and the camera body—a rigid machine quite unlike the porous stillness maintained in Simpson's story of the young girl.

The retinal image captured by the camera is presumably then transmitted to the brain, where it is somehow "processed" into knowledge about the thing being seen. This, Gibson argues, leaves unanswered crucial questions about how the brain deciphers the snapshot, and moreover, it is a far cry from how people actually see or how they know. The procedure of immobilizing the subject and measuring only one eye's functioning runs contrary to the way that humans as ambulatory beings perceive and experience the world. It also reproduces the Cartesian assumption of a static omniscient point of view from which the world can be known and described. The forced separation of eye from head and body goes against the kind of awareness of relationships for which Deloria and Kimmerer are advocating.

Barad also reinforces Deloria's observations about kinship and reciprocity by arguing for the impossibility of separating subject from object and the centrality of the enmeshment or entanglement of all things. While this entanglement implies an ethics of reciprocal relationality, Barad does not address the issue of respect directly, nor does Gibson. The ethics implicit in the practice of science that both Barad and Gibson break away from are based in the transparency and repeatability of a practice of experimentation, one that presumes the superiority of humans and objectifies the natural world. While they strongly disagree with the assumption that the world can be known by examining its isolable elements in a static place, they do not explicitly address the ethics of their approaches. I wonder if this is where the authors who have hung around so far part ways.

Strongly contrasting with standard forms of scientific inquiry and publication, Simpson emphasizes how patient observation builds connections that can be shared in ways that mutually benefit everyone. Ritual and ceremony are practices that can invoke and celebrate long-known connections, reminding and reaffirming participants' knowledge of them. They can also function to strengthen new connections and the relations they make possible.[44] Such practices offer an opportunity to dwell in the understanding of connection. As ways of making knowledge public, they perform how knowledge can only manifest as or from a collective endeavor.

Storytelling also functions to rekindle and animate knowledge, particularly about places and the events that happened in them. Stories are performed in places where people actively listen, tilting heads, closing eyes, rocking back and forth, breathing calmly or agitatedly, reaching out or clinging to one another. Storytellers typically emphasize certain words and react with facial expressions and shifts in position to the events being described, and listeners take these in along with the reactions of fellow listeners. Storytelling is thus an event that is shared and marked as such by all those in attendance. Unlike reading, which takes place as a more private and intimate exchange between book and individual, in which the book's weight and the lighting that helps make it more readable along with its position relative to the reader's head are central to the exchange, storytelling commemorates the sharing of events among people.

Keith Basso (Connecticut-based settler-scholar) describes the Western Apache custom of "speaking with names," in which storytellers use references to particular places to remind their listeners of past events. This enables listeners to imagine themselves in those places, to reinterpret what occurred there, and to glean insights relevant to their current situations. It also gives listeners the opportunity to add to the story themselves in their imaginations, thereby affirming that knowledge is continually constructed. Furthermore, as Basso would argue, placeless events cannot occur, and at the same time, places are alive with stories about the past. Places hold the memory of past events. In this way, the Land in which people live can be said to live in them. Van Dooren and Rose extend this argument across all species, arguing that storied spaces are multispecies achievements. Bats, penguins, and humans living around Sydney, Australia, each contribute to the making of different narratives about the nature of reality. Their actions are a form of narration, and envisioning them as such promotes a more reciprocal relationality.

Listening to these stories, attending to growth patterns, observing forms of interaction—building these connections is an ongoing practice. One does not achieve a permanent state of Hokowhitu's immediacy or Watts's place-thought. Rather, as I have emphasized, it requires an ongoing commitment to patient attention. Barad and Shildrick would argue that becoming individuated from all other matter is equally an ongoing process. The ethics embedded in the continual acknowledgment of those simultaneous actions of merging with and emerging from the world is likewise processual and requires continual reflection on the consequences of actions taken.

As I have stressed, both being and knowing result from bodily motion. Simpson's patient observation does not fix the body in place but instead asks for a continuing renewal of alertness through slight shifts of weight, perceptual focus, and gaze. The ball throwers who Chemero writes about know the distance to the target based on their proprioceptive sensations produced by previous and current motions. Standing, facing that target in the distance, they register the sense of fatigue in their arms by moving them ever so slightly at the same time that they assess the strength necessary to heave the ball. Ethical action in Simpson's example directs the young girl to observe the squirrel respectfully without intruding on its actions, and to presume it has knowledge to be learned. It would also direct the girl to share with her elders what she has learned and for them to consider her observations worthwhile. It might also entail thanking the squirrel at some future time by leaving it a gift. In the case of Chemero's ball throwers, it would not only include respectful treatment of them in setting up the task but also a discussion after the experiment that explained both the premise and the results so that the participants could learn how they contributed to understanding perception. Researchers might also reflect on their assumptions and carefully consider how their lab could better participate in respectful reciprocity.[45]

Practicing respect toward a squirrel or ball throwers involves establishing comfortable distances, appropriate forms of address (whether silence in the girl's case or appreciation in the researcher's case), and as Simpson insists, patience. To this I would reiterate that patience is, in part, a set of bodily actions—an attention to or feeling for another's state of being; an ability to read this from their actions, however subtle; and a capacity to restrain oneself, possibly making oneself smaller and less powerful in appearance or more open and receptive by softening the muscles or hollowing out the torso, suggesting a smile, adopting a softer tone of voice, and sustaining a quiet steadiness, all of which instantiate and demonstrate one's dedication to respect.

In case any of you are still here, thank you, authors, for letting me walk among and alongside you. I hope I haven't stepped on your feet or charged past, oblivious to what you stand for. I will keep trying on and trying out your thinking, all the while thanking you for your patience. I will also continue to try to imagine a world where all forms of knowledge-making and sharing—dancing, storytelling, experimenting, and philosophizing—are equally valid and valued not only for what knowledge they impart but also for the particular ways of knowing that they enable. It is also clear that not all knowledge should or can be shared. In many Native communities there are forms of knowledge, including dances, that are protected and not shared with any outsiders. Reminding myself of this deepens my understanding of how, when, and where knowing happens.

EMBODYING THE DECOLONIAL

In recent years, the term "embodied" has been used elastically to refer to anything from conservative ideas about how bodily action provides a format for neuronal representations or helps to reduce computational load, to a variety of "radical embodiment" proposals—for example, that kinesthetic body schemas are a constitutive part of mental skills, that sensorimotor know-how is a constitutive part of perceptual experience, that bodily life regulation is a constitutive part of phenomenal consciousness and its extended neurophysiological substrates, and that social sensorimotor interaction can be a constitutive part of social cognition. —EZEKIEL DI PAOLO AND EVAN THOMPSON, "The Enactive Approach" (2014)

The penchant to talk about and to explain ourselves and/or aspects of ourselves as embodied—as in "embodied connectionism" and even as in "embodied mind," "embodied schema," "embodied agents," "embodied actions," and "phenomenological embodiment"—evokes not simply the possibility of a disembodied relationship and of near or outright tautologies as in "embodied agents," "embodied actions" and "the embodied mind is part of the living body," but the spectre of Cartesianism. In this sense, the term "embodied" is a lexical band-aid covering a 350-year-old wound generated and kept suppurating by a schizoid metaphysics. It evades the arduous and (by human lifetime standards) infinite task of clarifying and elucidating the nature of living nature from the ground up. —MAXINE SHEETS-JOHNSTONE, "Emotion and Movement" (1999)

The past several years have witnessed a significant uptick in the number of times the adjective *embodied* is used. Pursued as part of the philosophical inquiries into phenomenology, especially since Merleau-Ponty's explorations of it in *Phenomenology of Perception*, the term *embodiment* has long been explored by feminist philosophers, including Simone de Beauvoir (unmarked), Iris Marion Young, and Sara Ahmed, and by many anthropologists influenced by phenomenology, such as Thomas Csordas (California-based settler-scholar).[1] The body also served as a key subject in feminist and women-of-color inquiries into public and private spaces and women's labor.[2] And it constituted a central theme for scholars working in queer theory and disability studies.[3] However, since 2000, the qualifier *embodied*, more than the body or embodiment, seems to have gone viral, attaching itself to a wide variety of terms to produce new categories of experience such as embodied agents, embodied research, and embodied memory. More specifically, new paradigms in cognitive science typically reference embodied memory and embodied cognition; various approaches to therapy speak about embodied spiritual growth, embodied care, embodied affective experience, embodied consciousness, and embodied clinical intuition; scholarship on education addresses embodied knowing, embodied inquiry, embodied teaching, embodied writing pedagogy, embodied engagement, embodied authority, embodied reflection, and embodied learning; architecture now includes embodied design ideation as well as embodied architectural design; and musicologists write about embodied composition and embodied music interaction. In the last decade, book titles indicating other categories of what is embodied include *The Embodied Performance of Gender, Embodied Power, Embodied Food Politics, Embodied Research Methods*, and *Embodied Protests*.[4] Additionally, and most recently, the adjective *embodied* has popped up in a variety of new social justice initiatives.

What can be deduced from this precipitous groundswell of attempts to emphasize the body's participation in various kinds of pursuits and practices? Perhaps the advent of digital technologies and the gargantuan increase in time devoted to screen culture has created a new need for the category of the embodied. Or perhaps no overarching motivation exists, and the drive to qualify experience as "embodied" stems from discipline-specific concerns. Cognitive science, for example, seems to have undergone a significant paradigm shift, reflected in the groundbreaking work of George Lakoff and Mark Johnson on cognitive linguistics as well as the substantial number of neuroscientists who have probed sensorimotor–brain connections only to discover that thinking and remembering take place across the entire body.[5] Referred to as "enactivist" or "ecological" cognitive science as well as "embodied cognition," scientists engaged in this new inquiry are themselves aware that referring to their approach as an exploration of "embodied" cognition fails to delineate adequately which aspect of mental life is being considered, as the epigraph from Ezequiel Di Paolo (unmarked) and Evan Thompson (unmarked) makes clear.

A related yet different set of motives appears to be fueling the use of *embodied* in gender and cultural studies broadly considered, and these motives may well be at work in therapeutic and pedagogical implementations of the term *embodied*. Stemming from Haraway's dedication to "situated or embodied knowledges," or Sandra Harding's (California-based settler-scholar) standpoint theory, the desire to specify the bodiliness of experience may signify an allegiance to forms of responsible, that is to say, locatable, knowledge and knowledge claims.[6] As Haraway notes, a pair of eyes looking out onto the world from a particular body can only have a partial and particular view of what is around them.[7] Thus, what is embodied cannot masquerade as universal, self-evident, or omniscient. Instead, knowing is always limited, coming as it does from specific contexts, each with its distinctive history. Sharing the understanding of gender as a constructed identity, a second group of scholars within gender studies deploys *embodied* to emphasize the protocols of comportment and other forms of nonverbal, normative behavior through which gender is established and maintained.[8]

A third implementation of *embodied* can be found in the work of scholars engaged with critical race and decolonial studies, whose use of the term may serve to signify resistance to white and settler-colonial structurings of knowledge that have ignored, suppressed, or marginalized ways of knowing that are highly valued within certain communities. Frequently referring to ritualized practices, dances, pageants, parades, and festivals, and also to more daily patterns and habits of moving through which knowledge is both shared and affirmed, this use of *embodied* stresses the importance of bodily action. As if in defiance of brain-based, logocentrically oriented knowledge claims, these scholars productively champion the patterning of movement through which valued ways of living are established and passed on to future generations.

In solidarity with all three of these efforts to emphasize the corporeal nature of experience, this essay focuses in detail on key terms to which the adjective *embodied* has regularly been applied—*practice, knowledge,* and *scholarship*. Along with cognitive scientists seeking to expand our understanding of what mind is, this essay considers various kinds of bodily participation in thinking. With scholars in gender and cultural studies, it also analyzes the myriad ways in which bodily movement participates in the formation of identity and the kinds of knowledge it makes possible. With performance studies scholars who are working to decolonize canonical conceptions of what knowledge is and where it is located, I aspire to affirm and support efforts to decolonize ways of knowing. As a longtime student of human movement, my hope is that this fleshing out of bodily action will contribute two kinds of insights: first, a greater awareness of movement itself and how to describe and analyze it, and second, an understanding of how the adjective *embodied* could continue to support a Cartesian epistemology that would perpetuate a patriarchal and settler-colonial relationship between something called "mind" and something called "body."

Every time I hear or read *embodied*, it conjures up the possibility of a disembodied version of the noun to which it is applied. Thus, the use of the qualifier *embodied* also suggests that there would be experiences or entities such as disembodied knowledge, disembodied practice, disembodied memory, or disembodied performances of gender. Is it the case, then, that the use of *embodied* does serve as a lexical band-aid, as Maxine Sheets-Johnstone (unmarked) argues in the epigraph. As a way to explore this question, I will attempt to detail the bodily actions that are presumably involved in practicing, thinking, and acquiring knowledge, supplementing these accounts with recent insights provided by research in neuroscience and sociology.

Following on from that discussion, I will consider the use of *embodied* in relation to the process of decolonization, arguing that suppression of the body's role in the construction of knowledge played an important part in the colonial project. In the same way that the land of the Americas was wiped clean of life and then parceled for ownership by its conquerors, so too, the body has been objectified with specific functions attributed to its individual parts, all in the service of sustaining and carrying the mind around.

Embodied Practice

The adjective *embodied* is attached to the noun *practice* in an astonishing number of academic, medical, and professional contexts, appearing most frequently in pursuits concerned with teaching, counseling, and forms of caregiving. The phrases *as embodied practice* or *and embodied practice* have been attached to nouns as diverse as *empathy, gender, video games, nation, religion, personal grooming, secrecy,* and *labor*. The intent in using the adjective comes across as the need to emphasize the body's role in these contexts, especially where it is often ignored, and yet the phrase seems almost as absurd as *embodied dancing*. *Practice* itself denotes the procedure for doing something or the application (through action) of a given idea, method, or theory. In its verb form, *practice* further reinforces the fact of physical action since it implies the repetition of patterned movement to improve proficiency or the regular exercise of a sequence of actions or a routine. What, then, is gained when *embodied* is added to it?

Although there seems to be no single response to this question, one answer might be embedded in the definition of *practice* itself as "a performance or application, a repeated or customary action, or the usual way of doing something."[9] This definition implies a separation between thinking and acting. If the regular actions that are part of the execution of an idea remain unseen and unacknowledged, perhaps because they are habitual or commonplace, then *embodied* might bring special attention to them or imbue them with greater significance. It could also reference a new set of actions or protocols that have been found to be more effective in addressing a given situation. Still, the use of *embodied*, while it emphasizes the centrality of the body's role, conveys little about the exact movement patterns or types of movement that are being implemented in practicing, for example, gender, nationality, or religious affiliation.

The notion of embodied practice is further complicated by the fact that *practice* references several distinct genres of activity. It signifies a custom or long-standing cultural observance usually performed by a group of people or the regularized commitment by an individual to improve one's performance at something, as in "How was practice today?" It also serves as the term utilized to describe a specific organization dedicated to specialized service, such as a medical, law, or counseling practice. In each case the application of *embodied* underscores what actions are entailed but in a slightly different way. Meditation, as a practice, implicates directly an individual or group in the act of meditation, whereas a medical practice references legal and other contractual restraints that conjoin a group of people together in providing health care.

Practices such as a reiterated ritual, celebration, or other form of convocation are all ways of collectively creating and re-creating social values. Identified by Diana Taylor (New York–based settler-scholar) as the repertoire in contrast to the archive, an instrument for colonial domination, these practices can be passed on through generations, always changing yet retaining their capacity to bring people together to reaffirm their common connections and shared orientation toward the world. As Taylor and many others argue, such practices contain and transmit knowledge, and as such they will be discussed in much more detail in the following section on embodied knowledge.[10]

Practice referring to an individual's repeated actions to achieve some desired outcome, what is often called "skill acquisition," seems always to entail physical activity as well as a tracking of that activity in terms of measuring or otherwise assessing the degree of change over time. Practice at a sport or with a musical instrument often unfolds according to designated stages of proficiency in which different types and levels of skill are achieved and then compiled. Different pedagogical models, each claiming to provide the most effective approach to training, highlight different aspects of the process of practice. *Embodied* can be used to bring attention to these singly or in combination.

Edward Baggs (unmarked), Vicente Raja (unmarked), and Michael Anderson argue that the body does change over the course of practicing, however such change is not registered in the body alone but rather in the interface between the body and its surroundings. Skills "arise always through situated engagement with an environment" and because of this they propose that *skill adaptation* and *skill attunement* are more appropriate terms than *skill acquisition*.[11] *Embodied* is sometimes used to emphasize this relationship between body and environment, either physical or social.

Similarly, in institutional settings such as schools, counseling centers, or care facilities, *embodied* highlights the bodiliness of the interactions taking place. It also sometimes connects a greater attentiveness to physical actions with the relative effectiveness of the practice. Bodies convey enormous amounts of information about peoples' capacities, limitations, preferences, tendencies, aversions, willingness, and sense of relation to one another. The fact that this has been ignored in so many training systems and that *embodied* needs to be utilized to encourage such attention is deeply concerning. However, even though *embodied* adds emphasis to bodily movements and activities, it also erases the specificity of those actions. While trying to throw light onto what bodies actually do, it renders opaque the physical processes and responses in which bodies engage by neglecting to describe them in any detail.

How, for example, does a teacher enter a room full of students—with a crisp closing of the door followed by a stern surveillance of the room, or a

Embodying the Decolonial · 61

casual saunter and nod to the group, or a lowered gaze and immediate preoccupation with the books being laid out on the desk? Each of these patternings of motion propose different kinds of relations between teacher and students. Similarly, a teacher's desk placed at the front of the room with all students seated equally spaced apart and facing toward that desk constructs an authority for the teacher that sitting in a circle where the teacher is just one of the contributing participants alters. What is accomplished in advocating for an embodied approach to teaching without detailing the teacher's manner of address or the spatial organization of the classroom?

The example of a teacher's demeanor and the spatial organization of the classroom is but one effort to delineate the many ways that embodied teaching could be analyzed and described. The fact that such details are so often passed over leaches movement of its capacity to articulate a stance or construct forms of identification and agency. Doesn't each embodied practice deserve to be fleshed out as a set of decisions made and performed by the whole person in motion?

Embodied Knowledge

Where "embodied" practice seems to focus on the ways that the body is implicated and involved in various pursuits, "embodied" knowledge emphasizes the fact that such actions are themselves forms of knowing. Such actions include the possible pedagogical styles with their habits and techniques of the body referred to in the previous section and also the larger social protocols of comportment and established ways of moving that Bourdieu named the "habitus." Ways of walking are established as signs of mood or manliness; pathways into and through a domicile are equally associated with gendered identity.[12] Each caste and class manifests ways of moving, speaking, gazing, and greeting, yet, as Bourdieu insightfully observes, these action patterns are, for the most part, unconsciously formed and preserved. Because of this, he argues, these daily movements seem improvised despite their systematic regularity.[13]

The meanings embedded in the habitus, in turn, inform the significance that practices such as rituals, ceremonies, pageants, and dances offer. As many researchers have shown, motions toward up and down, left and right, forward and back, the size of one's personal kinesphere, the design of a pathway through space, the speed, flow, rhythm, and a host of other qualities and ways of moving reinforce or differ from normative patterns so as to assert new knowledge and/or reinforce existing understandings of the world. Perhaps it is because these patterned motions are more consciously performed than other protocols that form the habitus that they acquire the qualifier "embodied." Or perhaps there is a perceived need to validate the body and its motions as capable of knowing and of knowing in a unique way.

A number of dance scholars have addressed the ways that dancing both creates and reaffirms knowledge, each focusing on a different aspect of this process. Yvonne Daniel (Black) has argued that specific ways of moving in Haitian Vodun, Cuban Yoruba, and Bahamian Candomblé articulate a relationship between the dancer and the spiritual world. The act of moving both enacts and preserves this relationship, fostering individual healing and health as well as forging strong connections among practitioners in their efforts to apprehend spiritual forces, either ancestral or cosmic, and to translate the wisdom of these forces into daily life practices. As part of the ceremonies that enable this worship, dancers learn to follow a choreography that invites spirit possession. When this harboring of divinity occurs, dancers' movement patterns shift dramatically and persist for an unpredictable period of time. Such radical changes in the dancing affirm the existence of the spirit world and provide lenses through which to contemplate social relations within the community. Daniel further illustrates how these belief systems became enmeshed once they left Africa and settled in the Caribbean, where they endure as distinctive iterations of Africanity. The dances thus gesture toward a spirit world and a knowledge base that originally formed in Africa.[14]

Differently, Cristina Rosa (Brazilian) traces the connection between West and Central African movement aesthetics and a Brazilian style of moving found in samba de roda, capoeira Angola, concert dance, and even soccer. The characteristic swaying of the hips found in all these practices, known as *ginga*, enables syncopated relations among legs, torso, and head. Introduced into Brazil via the slave trade and persisting across centuries of contentious negotiations around Brazilian racial and ethnic identities, *ginga* emerged in the twentieth century as a core aspect of national identity, allowing especially disenfranchised citizens the possibility "to both *recuperate* their sense of self-esteem and dignity and *invent* renewed identities that connect blackness to concepts such as grace and pride."[15] Like the choreographies of worship that Daniel describes, *ginga*, as a way of moving, enables one to apprehend at a bone-deep level core aspects of who one is.

Rosa, however, sees this assimilation and affirmation of knowledge as occurring within the colonial and postcolonial power relations that define Brazilian history. Knowledge as experienced through *ginga* and the sense of identity it yields cannot be separated from the power relations in which it is enmeshed.

Writing about Tewa dances of central New Mexico, Jill Sweet (United States–based settler-scholar) explains that their ceremonial dances provide the opportunity to come together to commemorate and renew community.[16] Serving as celebrations of the seasons and the animal and plant life that provide subsistence, they also reaffirm aesthetic preferences that include the appearance of group cohesiveness in which no individuals stand out as dancing harder or better.[17] Each of the dances performed at distinctive moments in the year combine lyrics, gestures, and spatial orientation to signify themes deemed central to Tewa identity. Through the buffooning behavior of clowns and other humorous elements, the dances can also specify clear directives for what is inappropriate.[18] Yet another function of the dances has been to provide opportunities to reflect on and readjust attitudes toward neighboring tribes, such as the Navajo, with whom the Tewa have sometimes been at war.[19] Through humorous stereotyping and cross-dressed impersonation of the Navajo, Tewa can relive a complex history of entanglement and opposition. The knowledge that dancing generates thus assists in articulating attitudes toward the dancers' world and their relations with it.

Where the Tongva were often displaced from their Lands, moved onto mission compounds, or pushed into other territories, the Tewa were able to remain on the territory settled by their ancestors, and this Land, with its defining mountains, rivers, and lakes, is often referenced in the songs and in danced gestures.[20] Although missionaries strongly prohibited and policed dancing in the early phase of colonization, they adopted a much more lenient policy after the successful uprising of 1680. In the early twentieth century, with the significant increase of Anglo tourists, the Tewa revised ceremonial dances for theatrical presentation, yet the village dances also persisted, and they have enjoyed increasing popularity in the twenty-first century as occasions to regather and collectively experience a shared knowledge of how to be in the world. Entailing complex sets of responsibilities that begin many days or weeks before the actual dance, they involve the entire pueblo population in roles that reinforce values around appropriate behavior.

Where the Tewa found ways to construct both tourist and ceremonial dances as efficacious, the Chumash found it necessary to form a sharp divide between sacred and tourist dances. Although heavily disrupted by missionization and the brutal crackdowns on ceremonial practices by Spanish soldiers and missionaries, some dances have survived among the Chumash, according to Weighill. Contrasting these sacred dances with the Orientalized and commodified "Indian dances" often seen onstage as tourist attractions, he suggests that the sacred dances that are performed manifest "the spirit world" and become "a way spirits show themselves in the material world."[21] In witnessing these dances, tribal members come to know the spirit world as much as the dancers do.[22] Although no longer located at the center of "families' theological, political, and sociological constructions,"[23] dance continues to hold a much-revered position within Chumash culture.[24]

Jacqueline Shea Murphy (California-based settler-scholar) theorizes the difference between tourist and ceremonial dances by pointing to the different assumptions held by settler colonists and Native peoples regarding the function of dance. Where settler colonists envision dance merely as a form of representation, a superficial and often superfluous depiction of events, Native dancers conceive of their movements as enactments that are capable of bringing into being the values and relationships that they are dancing. Shea Murphy complicates this distinction further by pointing to Native dancers' participation in Buffalo Bill Cody's Wild West show. At a time when Native peoples were prohibited by the US government from all practices of dancing, Cody and other settler-colonist entrepreneurs were hiring them to perform in their extravaganzas. In such situations, Shea Murphy speculates, Native dancers had the opportunity to enact their values despite the framing of the dances as mere entertainment. Yet the dancers also took advantage of the situation to assert a different kind of knowing by playing into and even exaggerating the Western stereotypes of themselves, thereby asserting knowledge about the colonizers of which they themselves were unaware.[25]

Today, as Native choreographers enter the proscenium theater, Shea Murphy argues, they open an interrogation of the assumption that performance is an ornamental diversion or superficial representation. Incorporating movement from yoga, modern dance, and other genres, they hold to an understanding that their dances are acting in, on, and with the world. Dancing thus articulates both knowledge and a way of knowing that makes its presence known and available to both dancers and viewers.[26]

Embodying the Decolonial · 65

The kinds of knowledge these authors describe are typically excluded from Western conceptions of what constitutes knowing. The dances do not produce facts but instead relationships with highly complex entities that are themselves in motion. The spirits invoked in Vodun, the Africanist aesthetics identified by Brenda Dixon Gottschild (Black) that persist in the Caribbean and Brazil, the mountains and rivers to which the Tewa pay homage, all continue to evolve alongside the dancers who move with them. The knowledge forged in these interactions, like the dancing itself, is transient, yet it can cause changes in the dancers' orientation within and toward the world that endure.

Each of these examples of danced knowledge also exemplifies a distinctive role for dance as well as a specific set of values that the dancing makes available. The dances can commemorate, celebrate, affirm, or contest assumptions about self and world. The examples also illustrate different forms of connection, whether to a spirit realm, a complex history of migration and assimilation, or one's local surroundings. In varying ways they open up spaces for reflection on the knowledge they are producing, whether through the spatial organization of the dancers, their humorous antics, or trance states of being. Many other activities also produce knowledge, however dance and the larger ceremonies in which it participates provide particularly complex and concentrated enactments of knowing.

The knowledge produced in dancing exists not only in the content but also in the content of the form that is being enacted. Knowledge dwells not just in the lyrics of a chant, for example, but also in the ways it is delivered: the rhythmicity, timbre, and tonal relationships that the singer articulates, the subtle swaying with its sequential articulation of spinal vertebrae, the placid or vibrant weightiness of the torso, the sudden or gradual shifts in direction for head, body, and feet. Whether performing for tourists or for one another, Tewa believe that the dances are effective when they are performed from the heart. This particular form of commitment enables the dances to bring beauty and connect, as Andy Garcia (Tewa) explains, to "the different creatures such as the buffalo, the dog, deer, antelope, elk, eagle, hawk, and turtle. Other dances pay respect to corn, clouds, trees—all of nature. Pueblos do not think of themselves as separate from nature or superior to other creatures. Of course, we do go to supermarkets, but we will not forget the ways of our ancestors. If we lose those ways, we lose ourselves."[27] Performing from the heart, as Garcia describes it, entails a full-bodied commitment to each action in which one's entire being is summoned into motion.

Dancing in all its complexity and simplicity of focus on the act of moving may exemplify one of the most robust practices of knowing, but returning to the question "What kind of knowledge is not embodied?" is there some kind of knowledge discovered or learned by the brain only (as if the brain were not part of the body)? Could there be knowledge achieved by the brain alone, isolated from the senses or the capacity to move in the world? How about mathematics? Long considered the most cerebral of all intellectual pursuits, mathematics has recently been studied by researchers trying to identify how it is learned.[28] They have observed the way that students learn to write equations, and in particular the way they space the various operations, such as multiplication and addition, delineated within a given equation. Without it ever being communicated verbally, students pick up a spatial strategy that makes it easier to see what they need to do with the various parts of the equation, clustering together the symbols for one kind of operation and spacing further apart symbols for another. Doing mathematics thus involves achieving the right perception of an equation, which, in turn, depends on bodily movement.

How different is the spacing in an equation from achieving the correct spacing among dancers in a given ceremony? The spacings are both meaning-filled acts even though they indicate very different kinds of meaning. They also each imply skill, or what is often called "know-how." One knows how to inscribe the parts of the equation just as one knows how to sense and adjust the distance to other dancers. The know-how involved in knowing thus makes evident the intrinsic connection between body and surroundings on which knowing is based.

Loïc Wacquant (California-based settler-scholar) seems to agree, arguing that people are "sensate, suffering, skilled, sedimented, and situated" creatures.[29] From before birth, humans are actively engaging with their surroundings, absorbing the limitations and affordances they offer. As Wacquant further argues, these "structures do not exist simply . . . in the form of invisible relations, objective distributions of resources, or systems of constraints and opportunities that press or limit them from without. They are also dynamic webs of forces inscribed upon and infolded deep within the body as perceptual grids, sensorimotor capacities, emotional proclivities, and indeed as desire itself. Structures are internal springs or propellers as much as they are external containers, beams, or lattices. They are limber and alive, not inert and immobile."[30] The techniques, habits, and protocols that compose sociality become routinized in neuromuscular action. They inform perception of what is possible, and in so doing, function as a corporeal episteme. They both are knowledge and make possible the acquisition of new knowledge. Unique to each physicality and shared, developed individually and collectively, these flexible repertoires of movement know and learn.

Embodied knowledge thus consists in specific patternings of movement that are learned and practiced and, through that assimilation into one's physicality, placed in the service of knowing. The details of these movement phrases, their spatial and rhythmic organization, and the forms of energy they summon into being all deserve detailed attention as part of the project of claiming that knowledge is embodied.

Embodied Scholarship

Finally, I would like to ask, "What it is that scholars do?" Barad, Vicki Kirby (Australia-based settler-scholar), and Jane Bennett (Maryland-based settler-scholar) all have argued that the acts of researching and writing issue from matter's capacity to reflect on and understand itself. Furthermore, scholarship is not conducted by an autonomous individual person but rather by multiple and complex interacting systems. As Bennett explains: "The sentences of this book also emerged from the confederate agency of many striving macro- and microactants: from 'my' memories, intentions, contentions, intestinal bacteria, eyeglasses, and blood sugar, as well as from the plastic computer keyboard, the bird song from the open window, or the air or particulates in the room."[31] While Bennett insightfully points to various forms of matter that participate in the generation of scholarship, I would add that the motion that ignites these interactions is equally important. In what follows, I outline a partial list of those actions, each of which could be examined in much further detail.

Scholars read using eyes or fingertips or ears, sometimes enunciating every word silently and other times scanning quickly across the page, holding the book or tipping the screen, adjusting the distance between image and eyes or between Braille and fingers or between speaker and ears. They readjust posture multiple times, stop to stare into space, scratch or pick at skin, take a sip of tea or coffee or water, stretch the neck, roll the shoulders, readjust again and continue this process. Fitting fingers to keyboard, or pencil, or tape recorder, they type, write, or speak notes from this reading, sometimes faithfully quoting phrases or sentences and other times, crafting a summary of what was read. They take a break, or search the internet for further references, compile a list of books to retrieve from the library, or find sources online that will augment further time spent scanning a screen. They travel to the library, haul books off shelves, organize them into stacks at a desk, hunt through them, thumbing pages slowly or quickly, in search of specific commentary that will contribute to a growing understanding of the subject. They go for a walk, gaining new distance or a new perspective, both literally and figuratively, on the topic, then return and jot down some notes, and often, reorganize the papers and books on the desk.

Scholars may also go out into the world, carefully observing surroundings along with the actions of people moving through them. Sometimes they talk to these people, asking them about their thoughts and feelings, their past experiences or aspirations for the future. They note relationships between bodies and spaces, sometimes photographing what they see or recording what they hear. Returning to their desks, they write up remembrances from these observations, study the photos, play back the tapes. The next day or the next, they do this again, and then again, slowly accumulating a deeper understanding of the structures and rhythms that help organize a given sociality. This allows them to ask new questions, to enter into more detailed conversations with people, and to make even more detailed observations about a shared world. Throughout this process, do they hold themselves slightly apart, maintaining an inkling of rigidity or stiffness to isolate themselves from the scene? Or do they immerse themselves in the action, going with the flow, embracing the unanticipated? Or perhaps they waver back and forth.

Invoking similar forms of interaction, they might also become students of a particular practice within the community, learning to wrestle, to do woodworking and carpentry, to participate in a musical ensemble, or to dance in a specific style.[32] As they learn, they watch themselves learning, noticing what is difficult or strange, unexpected or easy; making mistakes and then trying again, they also reflect on why they failed and when they succeeded, reiterating movement sequences, slowing them down, examining them in detail, so as to perfect them. Watching themselves building skills and developing a rapport with the teacher and with fellow students, they accumulate the reasoning underlying the "how" of each action so that eventually they acquire the tricks of the trade. They collect these insights and work to translate them precisely and vividly into words.

Additionally, they might conduct interviews with fellow learners in the class, members of the community being studied, or with specialists. In these interviews they try to notice the focus of the eyes, the feelings playing across the face, the shifts of weight and changes in postural configuration, the tapping of fingers or wringing of hands, also, the reluctance or enthusiasm, urgency or tentativeness with which any statement is delivered, the qualities of voice and breath, and how all these combine with the words being spoken to create specific meanings. They add the notes made about these conversations to the growing piles or folders or stickies, depending on how they physically organize their thoughts.

They design machines that extend the senses, enabling them to see further, hear more acutely, and probe more deeply into matter and space. They place these machines in the service of what-ifs, controlled situations in which it is possible to focus on causal relations between an action and a response, itself another action. Reconfiguring the controlled encounter and recalibrating instrumentation, they then perform the experiment again.

They journey to conferences and deliver papers, reporting on their research while also listening to presentations by colleagues, rolling eyes, applauding vigorously, or perhaps dozing off. They eat, drink, and gossip, catching up, getting new tips, making new alliances and discoveries. They hold roundtable discussions, watch films or lecture demonstrations, all the while aligning and comparing what they are taking in with their own research interests. Sometimes, they also present aspects of their research in the classroom, followed by questioning from students that can help further clarify understanding. In answering these questions, they again search the students' faces and bodies for signs of attentiveness, puzzlement, boredom, or comprehension. As in their interviews, they assess how the transmission of spoken ideas is going, attending to the translation of idea into speech but also watching and feeling kinesthetically how the message is both delivered and received. Are the students "grasping" the concepts?

And, finally, they write, mostly sitting, although sometimes standing while also squirming, stretching, straining, and rocking back and forth. They type or pen longhand a phrase or a sentence, pause, consider, reorganize or amend the words, stare out into space, lean to the side, as if to see the idea from a different angle, type some more. They reread what they have, add a little more, go off in search of a reference, reoutline the whole paragraph or page, delete, cut and paste, start again. They type more and press save, print out and scribble edits, cross out words, circle phrases, and add arrows indicative of their new location; they type those in and plow ahead. The act of writing reiterates many of the actions performed while reading—scratching, picking, smoothing; also propping the head on a bent arm, or cupping the chin with the hands; twisting, slumping, sighing, yawning; also removing a piece of lint from a garment or a crumb from the desk; pressing save again, just in case. The keyboard gets filthier and filthier; coffee is spilled, phone calls are made, email and texts are checked and sent. Writing includes wandering away, doing the dishes or the laundry, all the while thinking about being at the desk. Writing can entail getting anxious, disgruntled, or dispirited, and often, taking another pee break. Then scholars quit for the day, or, perhaps, squeeze out a few more sentences.

Sometimes phrases or whole sentences are formulated and then typed out. Other times writing takes place while the words are being developed. Sometimes, scholars spatially reorganize the sequence of thoughts in their imaginations, and other times, they use scraps of paper on the desk, jotting additional notes onto them. Sometimes they struggle to find the verb or adjective that precisely captures the idea or relationship they seek to describe. Days later, while rereading, the right word becomes evident. Sometimes they argue with themselves, criticizing ideas, silently or out loud. Then they start again or continue on, eventually pressing send.

The writing is received by editors who designate readers to evaluate it, and if it is deemed meritorious, it is processed by copyeditors and designers who format it for the printed page. It then circulates to a wider audience of readers who busily engage with the actions involved in reading (previously described). Opinions are formed; texts are sent. Someone somewhere thinks, "Wow, that changes my mind." And what is that changing of mind, if not a reconfiguration of one's physical stance and orientation toward the world that enables one to perceive anew? Perhaps new questions are asked and associations made, and, if so, how are these not part of a reformulation of the practices of reading, talking with people, and observing closely? Some of this writing finds its way into libraries and archives, where, again, scholars come to seek it out, check it out, and carry it home (as described earlier). Yet as I will discuss in more detail, despite the permanence and solidity that these institutions convey, it is the actions of all those circulating through them that construct what knowing, discovering, and proving are.

Embodying the Decolonial · 71

Having detailed to some degree what doing scholarship is, I am left asking, "What part of it is embodied and what part of it is not?" Are the reading and writing disembodied while the interviewing or participant observation qualify as embodied? What if we refuse to impose this distinction? What if all these actions are both thinking and doing?

Turning again to cognitive science, as Anderson argues, we do not think up an action in our minds and then execute it with our bodies. Rather, we move so as to achieve a desired effect. Furthermore, we do not perceive by measuring distances or calculating angles. We perceive throwability rather than weight; reachability rather than distance; and climbability rather than slope.[33] Thus, behavior is not the result of choosing the right response to a given stimulus, but instead achieving the right perceptions given the goal. A wonderful example of this can be found in the way that a baseball player catches a fly ball. Researchers have found that being in the right place to receive the ball has nothing to do with calculating the ball's speed or its parabolic curve as it rises, crests, and starts its descent, predicting where it will land, and then running there.[34] Players instead move to the place where they can no longer see the ball's acceleration toward earth. When the catchers can no longer see that it is accelerating, they are where it will land.[35] The ball affords catchability when the catcher is positioned so that it looks a certain way.[36] The running to the right spot, the spatial and postural adjustments, the raising of the arm, just like the mathematician writing the equation, are all part of the thinking.

I cite this example not to valorize cognitive science as providing a definitive or conclusive determination on the nature of mind, but rather to provoke further examination of how moving may be an intrinsic and essential part of thinking. What if going for a walk really does "get ideas flowing?" What if those ideas are not separate from the feelings that birthed them along with the proprioceptive sensations that were occurring as they were formulated? What if the various techniques for organizing desks and desktops consist of movements that help us understand how ideas are connected such that regarding where things are and moving them around are acts of thinking? What if all that scratching and stretching performed while writing helps focus concentration, thereby becoming integral to achieving the desired effect of producing a sentence?

Decolonizing the Disembodied

Thinking, learning, and remembering all involve bodily action every step of the way, and yet the body's integral participation in these activities has been, until recently, systematically ignored and suppressed. In the concluding portion of this essay, I put forward some speculative propositions about the connections between a disembodied framework for understanding knowledge and the project of colonization, specifically in the Americas. Operating within the Foucauldian notion of the episteme, I ask what kinds of bodily transformations were necessary to construct the colonizer to understand better what is entailed in decolonizing corporeality. Along the way I will consider how the movements involved in learning and sharing knowledge came to be disregarded or dismissed.

In his essay on epistemic racism and sexism in the long sixteenth century, Grosfoguel argues that multiple large and overlapping projects of colonization were launched by the Spanish that resulted in what he calls "epistemicides," defined as the systematic killing off of worldviews. Not only were the worldviews from Africa and the Americas destroyed along with the spiritual belief systems of Jews and Arabs, but also the knowledges stored in the bodies of women who were exterminated as witches during the Inquisition. As Grosfoguel observes, "The 'books' were the women's bodies," and, like the 500,000 volumes in the great library at Córdoba, they were incinerated.[37] Grosfoguel connects the destruction of these knowledges to the Cartesian separation of mind from body and its assertion that thinking takes place solely in the mind. Following Dussel, he further argues that the "monological, unsituated and asocial" production of knowledge that defines Cartesian inquiry was preceded by two earlier developments—conquest and extermination.[38]

Spain's rulers, having secured a Christian, patriarchal authority within the country's borders, financed explorer-soldiers to sail west, where they first encountered the Indigenous peoples of the Caribbean and subsequently the Aztecs. Armed with weapons, immunity to the diseases they carried with them, and, perhaps most crucially, the charge that they must bring the word of God to the "savages" they "discovered" in the "new" world, they began the process of reordering life and land to maximize access to vast quantities of precious stones, metals, and fertile earth. Claiming for Spain and then repurposing the land while also docilizing its inhabitants, they held to the belief that their actions were bettering the Native peoples they encountered.

As Wynter explains, the newly emerging subjecthood that the soldiers enacted, human centered and capable of conquest, was liberated from the God-ordered universe and became capable of exercising the principles of scientific observation as the central means of knowledge acquisition.[39] Nonetheless, this subject was dependent on the creation of an Other who would serve to justify the conqueror's isolated supremacy.[40] Wynter points out that Christopher Columbus learned the techniques for constructing this Other from Arab descriptions of West Africans that stereotyped those peoples as subhuman. Native peoples in the Americas were thus scrutinized along with West Africans, who were slowly introduced into the New World through the slave trade, to determine their capacity for and degree of humanness.[41] No single or consistent rubric of measurement prevailed; however, as Wynter argues, African slaves suffered most frequently from reduction to the category of fungible labor while Native peoples on the North American continent were often seen as idolators but salvageable.[42] It is this triadic model (white-Native-Black) rather than a dyadic model (white-Native) that needs to be implemented to understand fully the antagonisms that would bring forth the notion of the modern human and inform the project of conquest.

Examining conquest with attention to the bodily actions entailed, what would be required for the conqueror to dominate over the other person? It would seem he, and I use the masculine pronoun intentionally, must distance himself, still his body, and disengage from much of the information it is providing in order to presume an isolated and superior status. Through the utilization of certain classificatory principles based in measurements taken, and relying primarily on visual observation, he can then construct a difference between himself and others that can be used to rationalize his subsequent actions. Proclaiming discovery, the act of uncovering what was hidden or previously unknown, he implements an active-passive relationship in which what was unknown had no identity until it was discovered. Its existence then becomes assimilated into the regimes of knowledge exercised by the discoverer. He must say, "Your body and behavior are different from mine in ways that render it inferior." He must further say, "This land can and must be cleared, denuded of all entanglements between people and creatures, reconstituted as pristine blankness, and claimed so that it may be carved up and portioned out."

This classification of humans and other than humans into types, being based on the process of observing and evaluating abstracted features of their appearance and behavior, enabled Columbus to report to King Ferdinand II that the Native peoples he encountered would make excellent servants because of their physical appearance and their seemingly submissive responses.[43] Similarly, the partitioning of land depended on physical disengagement from it, accomplished by standing still on a rise in the land and looking out over it. It is likely that the surveyors either identified key landmarks, indicating a boundary by using them as markers, or they walked, counting steps or measuring the time it took to travel from one point to another.[44] The size of an apportionment of land was calculated in these ways, a process that implemented first stasis and then measurement as techniques for removing the observers from involvement with their surroundings. Such observers paid little attention to the kinds of relationships built among the various beings within the land, nor did they attend to what their bodies were doing when walking on the land. Parcellation was conducted almost exclusively through a conversion of space into metric units forming a grid, and it presumed the supremacy of the visual, as distinct from and superior to the other senses.[45]

Within this numerical regime, two kinds of labor were devised to realize the profits of conquest. The first disciplined bodies into the encomienda system, authorizing the conquerors to acquire large tracts of land and to extract forced labor from the Native peoples in exchange for which Native men were accorded a certain autonomy and responsibilities commensurate with their assimilation into Christianity. The second labor force, which Wynter argues is best described through the notion of the *pieza*, or interchangeable standardized quantities of the body's perceived capacity to work, was based in enslavement and ownership over bodies.[46] The idolators were seen as having a soul and hence eventually capable of conversion to Christianity, whereas those circulating through the economy as slaves were largely envisioned as subhuman. Although Dussel argues that annihilation and enslavement preceded Cartesian theories of cognition, the forms of thinking required to execute the actions described here seem to imply that a transformation already dependent on unsituated and asocial knowledge was well underway in the early years of colonization.

Thus, rather than inaugurating a new foundational understanding of knowledge production, Descartes may have been giving expression to epistemic assumptions that had already consolidated. His ego cogito, like the conquistadors, sequestered itself away from both its surroundings and its own physicality. The Cartesian way of knowing reduced physicality to a mechanics to be commanded by the mind, constructing a partition between objective and subjective stances toward the world, supported by expanding technologies of surveillance and measurement. A fragile and hence intensively defended illusion, objectivity could only seem to be achieved by the observer who held himself above, apart, and motionless. Yes, from a hilltop, the act of surveying one's surroundings can, perhaps, impart a sense of mastery over them, but anyone who has walked or ridden through hilly country knows that this sense of mastery is ephemeral and can only be achieved by being motionless. As soon as one moves, the surroundings change and take on, often, radically different appearances in relation to the viewer. Clearly, the stilling and silencing of the body is not the only factor enabling the act of conquest, yet it does play a central role in fortifying the superior positionality of the conqueror.

The armoring of physicality that is made possible through rigid stillness is what precedes and permits the kinds of violent acts of destruction and erasure that colonization executes. Such severing of physicality from its surroundings is built up slowly through simple acts, such as putting on boots, and deployed both slowly and suddenly. Painstakingly unknotting or quickly shattering connectedness, colonization individuates and isolates. The body re-forms as separated and segregated—placed within a hierarchy that prescribes what kinds of associations, but never connections, are possible.

All the while this is happening, there is a simultaneous erasure of the physicality involved in sorting, separating, and categorizing—a repression of how measurements are taken and recorded, attributes counted and assessed, whips or rifles raised, land grants signed, orders issued, surveillance performed, and a host of other actions that destroy relations that have been built over millennia. With geometrized space and quantified time replacing symbiotic practices of kinship, a self-validating system of accounting for the world emerges in which ownership takes precedence.[47]

Not only is the land owned, so is the body. Hands become "my" hands, legs, "my" legs. "I" becomes a small yet powerful and willful entity fed by the heart but located in the head. It tells the rest of what it senses around it to do things for it: Go get this, get better at this, get ready to go, get ahead, get it. And with each proclamation of getting comes a further denial of how the body got it, much less how community is possible.

What does this say, then, about the adjective *embodied* and its current popularity? On the one hand, *embodied* registers the effort to leave behind the Cartesian episteme along with the capacities to conquer, classify, and control that it enables. On the other, it seems to propose a distinction between forms of experience in which the body participates and those in which it does not play a role. If this is the case, then every time we write or read the adjective *embodied*, we must understand that we are simultaneously resisting and reinscribing a colonial understanding of the world.

REMEMBERING DANCING

This essay asks a lot of questions and provides very few, if any, answers. Chief among these questions is "What are we doing when we remember a dance, one that we have done or one that we have watched?" A second equally pressing question to be asked is "How do we remember dancing?" That is, what are the mechanisms of remembering through which we reach into the perceived past and reproduce dancing? Or, is that even what we are doing when we claim to be remembering a dance or a moment of dancing? Yet a third question might be "Why do these questions matter?," to which the provisional answer might be that they promote inquiry into how knowing happens through moving, by examining what remembering, a form of knowing, is. It also allows speculation about whether or how moving can know itself.

Paul Connerton (unmarked) proposes a distinction between social memory and individual memory, citing as examples of individual memory the memories of one's past life; of specific places or events, such as the layout of a city or the telling of a joke that are no longer attached to the specific moments of learning them; and the generalized ability to reproduce a certain performance, such as riding a bike or reading a book.[1] Yet, as Rolf Pfeifer (unmarked) and Josh Bongard (unmarked) make clear, these are only very broad categories, which, when considered in more detail, contain myriad distinct types of memory that include memory for vision, sound, smell, or taste (and here I would also add touch and movement); and also additional distinctions such as

> episodic memory (for personal experiences), semantic memory (for general knowledge), propositional memory (similar to semantic memory, for facts, objects, and people), autobiographical memory (recollec-

tions making up one's personality), flashbulb memory (specifically vivid memories, typically from emotionally charged situations), prospective memory (concerned with when something should be remembered, as in making a mental note) and retrospective memory (concerned with what should be remembered), procedural memory (for know-how, programs on how to do things), memory for sensory-motor skills such as driving a car, playing tennis, and juggling (which is related to procedural memory), declarative memory (for facts), and so on and so forth. These various types of memory are strongly intermixed. For example, a person's memory of the sight and sound of a Yamanote Line train in Tokyo (sensory memory) is associated with the memory of that person's last visit to Tokyo (episodic memory), which in turn makes up part of the individual's personality (autobiographical memory), and the meaning of the term Yamanote Line train (semantic memory).[2]

Reading through this exquisitely detailed yet daunting list, I remember each type of memory the authors identify. It presents an overwhelming number of ways that dancing might function in various forms of remembering.

Further complicating this list is the question of whether the distinction between individual and social memory is even a viable one. Many Native perspectives on memory do not envision the two as separate because each act of remembering issues from and forms part of a collective reservoir of knowledge. Like the Western Apache practice of speaking with names, in which places hold the memory of events that occurred there, memory is both shared and re-created in each individual act of remembering. As Basso documents, the names given by the ancestors refer to places where particular events, known by all members of the community, took place. These events represent aspects of ancestral wisdom.[3] If they are spoken of to a particular individual, that person will remember certain aspects of the event that are pertinent to their current situation in a way that will enable that person to reflect on their current situation or predicament and feel supported by the group speaking the names. As Lola Machuse (Western Apache) describes one such gathering: "We gave that woman [i.e., Louise] pictures to work on in her mind. We didn't speak too much to her. We didn't hold her down.... We gave her clear pictures with placenames. So her mind went to those places, standing in front of them as our ancestors did long ago. That way she could see what happened there long ago. She could hear stories in her mind, perhaps hear our ancestors speaking. She

Remembering Dancing · 79

could reknow wisdom of our ancestors."[4] Although the knowledge of the story is communally shared, each person's remembering of it will vary depending on what their present situation calls for.

Similarly, Native dancers may offer solos during a ceremony, however, as Weighill explains, they are never seen as dancing alone.[5] Each dance is envisioned as contributing to the entire ritual, one that is always collective. Furthermore, viewers, in a sense, dance along with the soloists as well as the groups through the quality of attention they share with the dancer on the dancing. These forms of collective action, as I argue throughout this book, enable groups to remember, sustain, and preserve their values.

While retaining the suspicion that the distinction between individual and social memory may obscure vital aspects of what memory is and how it works, the bulk of this essay focuses on new conceptualizations of the individual mind and of the mind-body relationship that are being developed in "ecological" or "enactivist" cognitive studies.[6] Subsequently, I will consider new theories of memory that are emerging as a result of ecological approaches, theories that very much resonate with the Western Apache practice of speaking with names. In a third section of this essay, I will reckon with some of the implications of this research for dance and dancing by mostly asking questions. A final brief section considers the role of dance studies within the Academy and asks whether it is helping to decolonize knowledge transmission and production. How does that sound?

Moving as a Form of Thinking; Thinking as a Form of Moving

As neurobiological mapping of the nervous system has continued over the last several years, a new thesis concerning what constitutes the mind is emerging, one that foregrounds the centrality of sensorimotor feedback loops to all forms of thinking.[7] This thesis grounds thinking in the continual back-and-forth between acting and perceiving (and perceiving as a form of acting). Thus, cognition is being reconceptualized as a capacity that is both distributed and interactive. Thinking is not a process that takes place in the brain but instead is accomplished through and across the combined neural, muscular, and perceptual systems. Additionally, it occurs through continual engagement with one's surroundings. How does this work?

As discussed in previous essays, perceiving and knowing are deeply entwined, connected through the act of moving and the proprioceptive information it generates. Both the body and the world are in continual flux, and only by synthesizing sensory and kinesthetic information is it possible to decipher and negotiate one's surroundings. At the same time, the physical structure of the body exhibits a morphological intelligence, that as Barrett explains, implies that "behavior is an actual constituent of a mind" and not a manifestation of what an internal mind is calculating.[8] Furthermore, as Anderson argues, actions are not thought up and then executed. Every action creates new intelligence.

The implications for cognition resulting from these kinds of findings suggest that the brain functions more as a coordinator of various forms of information, and that information changes continually as one moves throughout the day, interacting with others and with the environment. Each new moment presents opportunities for and challenges to sense-making, such that the brain is less a stable source of understanding and comprehension and more a processor capable of lightning quick improvisations. Anderson describes it this way: "Our brains are controllers capable of marshaling various internal (memory for abstract contingencies), physical (pencil and paper and the skills to use them), and sociocultural (formal and natural language) resources that together can generate Turing machines (or their functional equivalents) on the fly."[9] This description emphasizes the motionality and mutability at the center of cognition. Thinking is not the act of constructing a representation of events followed by a willful response. Instead, thinking consists of multiple processes of assessment based on the affordances available, and as these continually change, so do the "Turing machines" that enable people to effectively engage with the world.

In sum, the ecological thesis of cognition displaces notions of brain as storehouse in favor of a model of brain as improvisor, responding to the many kinds of information it is synthesizing at each moment. The brain forms but one part of a system of intelligence that is distributed across the body and extends out into the world. This intelligence is built into bodily structure as well as into the neuromuscular circuits that extract information and achieve desired perceptions of and orientations within our surroundings. If this is what thinking is and does, what is remembering, and how does it happen?

Ecological Remembering

As part of his efforts to analyze and understand memory, Marcel Proust (unmarked) examined the capacities and limitations of what he calls "voluntary memory." Assuming a separation between intellect and bodily sensation, Proust's voluntary memory repeatedly tried yet failed to yield specific memories of the town where he spent his childhood, yet his former surroundings became immediately available to him after the taste of a madeleine, a childhood favorite. He continues, "It is the same . . . with our own past. In vain we try to conjure it up again; the efforts of our intellect are futile." Drenched with affect, the past "'is somewhere beyond the reach of the intellect'—that is to say, of the voluntary memory—'and unmistakably present in some material object (or in the sensation which such an object arouses in us.)'"[10] What Proust describes is the relationship between memories of the past and specific engagements with our surroundings in the present. It is those tastes, sounds, or ways of moving that summon memory.

Recent experimentation points the way toward the neurophysiological basis for Proust's account. A remarkable study with an artificial mouse by Simon Bovet (unmarked) demonstrates how memory is located in the relationship between body and environment. The mouse, consisting of three kinds of sensors, one tactile, one visual, and one that registers a "reward," is placed in a simple T-maze that has two kinds of markers, one, a red wall along the top of the T, and the other, a pole located variably to the right or left at the junction between the vertical and horizontal parts of the T. A "treat" is placed at one end of the top of the T, and its location changes randomly but always in sync with the pole. As the mouse sets out, it registers the red directly ahead, and then when it turns, it either senses or doesn't sense the pole. Coming to the end of the top of the T, having chosen to turn either right or left, it may or may not find the treat. The experiment is repeated numerous times, with the result that eventually, the mouse starts consistently to make the correct choice about where the treat is located. This occurs because it learns over time that the coordination of pole on the left and wall on the right will produce the treat at that end, whereas when the pole is moved to the right and the mouse turns right aligning the wall to its left, the treat will be there.[11]

Pfeifer and Bongard explain that traditional theories of memory assume that the mouse would need to make a mental map of the connections between wall, pole, and treat, which would then be consulted before each decision to turn, yet the mouse has no neural capacity with which to construct or consult such a map. Instead, the mouse simply registers the conjoined sensations of the three sensors.[12] Thus, they argue, the memory needed to accomplish the task is located in the mouse's equivalent of visual, haptic, and gustatory sensation. If Proust spent his childhood in Illiers eating madeleines, as it seems he did, then it is entirely possible for their taste to provoke other memories of that place and time.

Numerous other studies expand on this basic insight concerning what memory is and how it works. Building on extensive experimentation that establishes connections between posture, facial expression, and memory recall, Katinka Dijkstra et al. (unmarked) measured the speed at which participants could retrieve memories when placed in postures congruent with the activity in the memory as opposed to postures that were unrelated or contradictory to the actions in the memory being recalled. Their findings show that recall was more likely as well as faster when congruent postures were assumed.[13] Confirming the introspective experience that memorizing is frequently accomplished through repetition, other studies have shown how sensory-motor encoding is integral to remembering sequences of numbers and lists of actions as well as past actions.[14]

Another kind of evidence for sensory-motor involvement in remembering comes from the long-standing method of loci, commonly known as the memory palace. Documented in early Greek and Roman texts on rhetoric, the method of loci is a technique for memorization that entails placing successive items to be remembered in specific locations in an imagined room, building, or along a street. Difficult to remember sequences, such as randomly generated lists of numbers or faces and names of strangers, are placed one by one in specific locations within the imagined site. Retrieval of the sequences is then accomplished by envisioning that one is walking through the site and seeing the items sequentially in their places. This envisioning of the walk activates ever so slightly the actual muscles used in walking and locating the objects. The imagined (yet actual) physical actions of walking and encountering objects in their designated locations yields a far greater rate of accuracy in recalling sequences. Like the artificial mouse that encodes memory in its sensors, the projected physical action of walking enables proprioceptive and visual sensors to synchronize the imagined place with the object to be recalled.

First elaborated in Marcus Tullius Cicero's (unmarked) *De oratore* and Marcus Fabius Quintilian's (unmarked) *Institutio Oratoria*, the method of loci was used regularly within the medieval Christian church and promoted heavily by Thomas Aquinas (unmarked). The Italian Jesuit Matteo Ricci (unmarked) used the technique successfully in China, impressing the court there with his abilities to remember random sequences of numbers during his stay from 1582 to 1610.[15] Although falling out of fashion in the eighteenth and nineteenth centuries, it continued to be incorporated into manuals on rhetoric and public speaking, where it was lauded as an effective technique for remembering the sequence of an argument. Interest in the technique has recently resurfaced as part of cognitive studies on memory where experiments using on-screen and VR versions of memory palaces also make evident the role of imagined walking in successful recall. Eric Krokos (unmarked) has shown that aspiring memorizers who use flat-screen versions of memory palaces are far less successful than those who are able to "stroll" through the palace using virtual reality technology.[16]

The fact that even when people only imagine moving through the memory palace recall is improved is based neurologically in the ways mirror neurons and other synaptic pathways activate the musculature at an almost undetectable level.[17] When one thinks of moving in a certain way, the muscles necessary to accomplish that action mobilize ever so slightly. These connections between imagining and moving have been utilized in a variety of therapeutic situations and also in sports science to rehearse and repattern action. Why not conceptualize these imperceptible kinds of muscular activation as a kind of thinking?

Experiments with robots, memory palaces, and other measurements of recall demonstrate the strong connections between sensorimotor activity and the process of remembering. Reflecting on these connections, many scientists working with the ecological cognition thesis are reexamining what memory is really for. Arthur Glenberg (unmarked) argues that memory facilitates our ability to mesh together the perceived properties in an environment and the conceptions we hold about those properties based on past experiences of them. According to Glenberg, what the environment affords, in Gibson's sense of the term, continually coordinates with the action patterns produced from past engagements with these affordances. In order to interact effectively with their surroundings, humans need to, for example, see the glass of water on the counter, determine its reachability and pick-up-ability, and connect that information with the amount of water previously consumed in the day, or their degree of thirst, or the pleasure that drinking water typically brings, or all of these. What matters, according to Glenberg, is that memory allows people to synthesize these various patterns of action, some in the present and some from the past.[18]

Using the example of finding the path home, Glenberg first considers how humans mesh current sensorimotor information about vegetation, soil and rocks, and the absence of low-hanging branches in order to conclude that, yes, this is a path. As one proceeds along it, further confirmation that it is the right path occurs through continuing to synthesize new perceptual information with past patterns of action, such as crossing a stream. Memory also updates as one encounters the trunk of a tree newly fallen, requiring the walker briefly to leave the path to get around the tree. It updates again as the path widens out into a field at the end of the forest.

Another set of observations offered by Israel Rosenfield (unmarked), Gerald Edelman (unmarked), and others attempts to account for the fact that, since everything in people's lives is continually changing, there are endless versions of a person or place. So, which or what is actually remembered?[19] The thesis that humans store an exact copy of someone's image in their brains does not help explain what is recalled when remembering someone. Rather than a procedure through which a stored copy is matched to what is currently seen in order for individuals to remember who or what it is, these researchers see memory as a form of categorization. Thus, Edelman asserts: "Memory is the enhanced ability to categorize or generalize associatively, not the storage of features or attributes of objects as a list."[20] Memory serves to sort out experience, enabling people to negotiate the enormous complexity of the world around them. Connecting this to Glenberg's thesis, it is not the conditions of the path on any given day that one recalls in trying to determine if it is the correct path. Rather, it is the generalized affordances it offers that allow a meshing of past with present.

If memory enables humans more effectively to engage with the environment, how could misremembering be accounted for along with the vast number of ways in which people remember inaccurately? Acknowledging the overwhelming number of things that might be remembered about an event, and also observing how places and people are constantly changing, Felipe De Brigard (unmarked) proposes that misremembering could serve to provide psychological and emotional support or assist in planning the future. He argues that memory functions as a form of hypothetical or speculative thinking about what might have happened or what might happen. He concludes that recent experimentation suggests that the mechanisms underlying our capacity to remember personal past events are integrated within a larger system that supports thoughts of what could happen to us in the future as well as what could have happened to us in the past. Furthermore, the reviewed evidence gives us reason to believe that the very cognitive system by means of which we operate with mental contents about personal events that did happen, also allows us to process mental contents about events that we think may happen or that we think could have plausibly happened in our lives. Remembering, therefore, may be best understood as a particular operation of a larger cognitive system that enables us to entertain episodic hypothetical thoughts.[21]

Seen in this way, remembering or misremembering can help people tailor future responses so as to avoid certain outcomes and achieve others.

This thesis concerning what memory is bears some resemblance to the Western Apache practice of speaking with names. Analogous to all the research confirming the intimate relationship between body and place, speaking with names situates specific events in certain locations. Because individuals have traveled to each location and been told what happened to an ancestor while there, the location itself, like the madeleine or the memory palace, ignites the memory. Also, the events associated with given places can be variously interpreted, enabling the person doing the remembering to sort through experience, simultaneously looking back at what the ancestors established and also forward to how these actions might inform one's own situation. Even more, they assist with the hypothetical thinking that De Brigard is describing by enabling individuals to try out various responses to a current predicament that could initiate a new course of action.

Relatedly, Pfeifer and Bongard argue that memory is detected as a change in behavior. We know someone has remembered something because of what they do. From this perspective, as in the example of the artificial mouse, memory is distributed across brain, body, and environment. It is locatable only in sets of relationships between individual, action, and surroundings. Rather than sitting inside the brain, memories are continually constructed through engagement with the world. Pfeifer and Bongard suggest as a metaphorical representation of memory the workings of a fountain. They explain: "What appears like a structure to the outside observer might be dynamically created, just like a water fountain whose bell-shaped appearance is not stored as a structure inside the fountain, but is emergent from the interaction of the shape and direction of the jets, the pressure at which the water is ejected, the surface tension of the water, and gravity acting on the water: it looks like a structure but is continuously created; it isn't 'stored' anywhere."[22] Presumably, the composition and organization of people's muscles, bones, and connective tissue would be the equivalent of the jets that propel water into the air, where it interacts with wind currents as well as gravity, and the water is like perceptual intelligence. The apparent objecthood of the fountain results from its continual in-motion-ness.

One drawback to this analogy between memory and fountain, however, is the fact that fountains are stationary and not particularly interactive. Human memory, in contrast, is always on the move. Memory is continually constructing itself through and in response to the movements individuals are making. It is produced through their sensory and muscular actions, even when those actions are virtually undetectable by them. Memory also responds to movements by meshing and updating new perceptions of the world with those from the past. For the fountain metaphor to work, it needs to be imagined as producing a visible structure, but one that is always transforming in shape as it moves through the world. Furthermore, this structure is highly pliable and continually responding to all the forms of engagement with which it comes into contact. Children splashing in it, animals and birds dropping by for a sip, a sudden rainstorm, wintertime temperatures—all these events remold and reshape the fountain, sometimes with lasting consequences.

Archiving Dancing

The studies of memory previously discussed focus on the important role that sensorimotor systems play in activating autobiographical memories. They make a strong case for a dance as a set of neural patternings that is not "stored" in the brain and then reconstructed, but instead distributed throughout the sensorimotor pathways that the dance originally activated. At the same time, they raise the question of what happens when the memory one is recalling is itself a form of movement. Is the case of remembering a dance a form of autobiographical memory or is it, following Connerton's typology, a case of activating more generalized abilities to reproduce a certain performance such as catching a ball, riding a bicycle, or reading a book? Or is it both?

Anecdotal ruminations on the subject offered by some of my colleagues suggest, in part, a distinction between dances that specify very precisely the exact bodily shaping, timing, location, and facing for each phrase of movement as contrasted with choreography that provides instead broad parameters for how to move but does not specify how dancers might respond to those parameters in detail. In those cases where dancers practice repeatedly the same sequences of movement, could it be the case that the form of memory that is established is the equivalent of the artificial mouse, who, once the appropriate synapses have coincided in becoming activated, does not forget which way to turn to get the treat? That is, dancers often report that they can remember years later their parts in dances that were practiced and performed hundreds of times. This would be the equivalent of autobiographical memory. Would the same hold true for the ability to access vocabularies of dance genres, such as steps frequently practiced in tap dance or ballet or various communal forms in which one may have trained extensively? Similarly, classical traditions of dance from South and East Asia, such as Bharatanatyam, Odissi, Khon, Indonesian court dances, and Chinese opera, require daily repetitive exercises over many years of study to build reflex-like patterns of action. Not unlike learning and then retaining the skill of how to ride a bicycle, these movement patterns live a long life in the body.

It is important to note, however, that when they develop skills through intensive repetition, dancers are not acquiring those skills, or coming into possession of them, within their individual and isolated bodies. Instead, the repetition of the actions serves to reorganize the entire system connecting the dancers to their environments. As Baggs, Raja, and Anderson argue, skills, like affordances, are located neither in the person nor in the environment, but rather in the interface between them.[23] Like the know-how discussed earlier, skills are forms of interaction that adapt to situations as they change.

In the same way that people can suddenly recall the full song or additional lines from a poem by repeating the phrases they do remember, so, too, rehearsing sections from a dance may enable dancers to continue dancing portions they might have forgotten. Such information is provided by sensorimotor pathways. However, could other kinds of sensation also assist? When dances involve partnering work, for example, does the added information concerning when and how dancers touched one another, how much weight and support they gave or received from one another, the direction and intensity of a push, grasp, clutch, slide, or shove inform them in remembering what came next? Again, like the mouse, the combination of visual, tactile, and kinesthetic information literally is, and thus provides, the memory. Does music offer similar assistance? If so, then examples such as these make especially evident both how memory is distributed across all the senses and also how integrative of them it is.

Dances that are built from prompts or directives or that unfold as a process may have left less of a trace in the senses and thus be more difficult to recall. Since their performance may have entailed improvising some or all of the choreography, what might be remembered is the sequence of types of activities, tasks, or scenes, each organized around specific constraints concerning where and how to move. Equally, the quality of attentiveness to other dancers, the sense of collective focus, the shared breathing patterns, or the feeling of moving together into a new section is what may be recalled.

Even these forms of choreography, however, usually rely on training regimens that have left deep imprints of action patterns in the body. Whether these regimens focus on breath, on one's relationship with gravity, or on maintaining an openness and responsiveness to events as they are evolving, haven't they given definition to a dancer's physicality and mobility in ways that are difficult, or even impossible, to forget?

Like moving interactive fountains, memory is shaped from birth along regularized channels of movement habits—prescriptions and proscriptions for when and how to move are abundant, if not consciously perceived. How quickly to move, how close to be to others, how abruptly or calmly to respond; when and how to sit or stand, lead or follow, give way, march ahead, relax, be alert, touch something or someone, stare or avert one's gaze, smile, clap, greet, ignore, hug... another endless list. Blended with these are protocols regarding proper performances of gender and other forms of social identification. All these habits and patterns are additionally infused with the effects of any forms of exercise in which the body participates— gymnastics, somatics, swimming, yoga, as well as any and all forms of dance training. A dancer brings trace memories of all these practices into the moment of remembering any dancing.

What does this say about concepts such as "muscle memory"? In one sense it validates dancers' and athletes' long-standing claims to be able to access memories of past ways of moving as stored in the musculature. In another, the very fact of specifying something called "muscle memory" reveals the extent to which theories of memory based on the brain as a system for storage and retrieval have long prevailed and claimed to be authoritative. It is not that there is one type of memory, known as muscle memory, in which deeply routinized patterns of motion are retained, and other forms of memory that reside in synaptic circuits stored in the brain. Rather, memories of any kind are hardly possible without some level of sensory-motor activation. Furthermore, if memory is in any sense "stored," it is housed in the entire body.

This, then, leads to the questions: "In what sense is the body an archive?" or even, "When is the body not an archive?" Defined principally as a place that contains public records about the past, the archive offers an interesting perspective on memory and body, and the new theories of memory previously discussed also provoke a reevaluation of what the archive is and does. Arguably, the learning of patterns of movement is most often a public event. As stated earlier, when people are learning to dance, they are also learning to walk, run, and locomote in a variety of ways, all of which are assimilated through imitation of others' actions. As Marcel Mauss (unmarked) has shown, these ways of moving, or as he calls them, "techniques of the body," are culturally and historically specific.[24] The ways that the body grasps, climbs, sits, or lies down archive the culturally distinctive actions of a group of people as well as the individual interpretations and adaptations made by each member. The body records and stores, in the form of habits of action, these fundamental patterns of society.

Likewise, learning to dance most often takes place in public and, at the very least, it is an interactive, social event. Bodies hold knowledge of dancing along with all the other habits of comportment, techniques for how to move, disciplinary prohibitions against moving in certain ways, and expressive possibilities for action they have assimilated and routinized over the years as sensorimotor pathways. Undoubtedly, these various holdings, or what might be called "documentations," of action interact with and influence each other. Ways of moving that have been incorporated prior to dancing also influence choices made about dance genre and movement style. For example, ways of performing gender could blend with ways of learning dancing or with inhibitions about moving in certain patterns or with certain parts of the body. Motifs of moving assimilated from one's parents or friends could merge with preferences for movement sequencing or quality. In this way, perhaps the body is not like an archive, since there are no clearly demarcated classificatory frameworks through which these various forms of knowledge are organized in relation to one another.

In many other ways, however, the body does function as an archive, not only housing documentation for how to move, but also how those who came before moved. People absorb what has sometimes been called "tacit knowledge" simply by being adjacent to those performing particular activities, some of which have descended to them through generations. Skills at cooking, for example, are often learned by children simply from watching others cook. As Luce Giard (unmarked) explains, these skills are not actively known.[25] At some point, when needed, they suddenly come into play. Ways of stirring, handling dough or a frying pan, tasting broth, and a host of other procedures involved in putting a meal together are often passed down. In some cultures, dances are similarly transmitted across generations, with children learning by watching and imitating. The learning of such dances can be in the service of preserving what Connerton calls "social memory" and Taylor refers to as "the repertoire." However, the incorporation of such knowledge by individual bodies takes place regardless of whether there is a social drive to archive dances through the organization of regular performances of them.[26]

If the body functions as an archive for both individual as well as some social memories, what might this tell us about what we have traditionally called "the archive"? The long-established conception of the archive as a permanent storehouse of lasting information about the past is strikingly analogous to the notion of the brain as a storehouse for memory. In both cases they are accorded ultimate authority and serve as arbiter of what the past was. Together they represent the epitome of Cartesian colonial operations that establish a stronghold of certainty that is uncontaminated by physicality and hierarchically superior to it.

In contrast to this mind-body separation, and in line with recent developments in cognitive science, I would argue that the way the archive functions is more like Pfeifer and Bongard's memory as fountain. Rather than a storage facility, the archive is an interactive site where people continually engage with traces of the past to produce new meaning in the present. Materials are brought into the archive by people who have stumbled over them in their attics, basements, garages, or flea markets. These documents are examined by people who make a determination as to their worth and classifiability. They are then sorted and filed, packed away in certain locations within the archive where they are from time to time retrieved and carted to tables where readers await them. These readers have scoured the catalogs in search of specific documents, but frequently miss something, so their requests lead to one kind of understanding and not another. They also spy something being studied at an adjacent table, get a tip from one of the librarians, or fail to find something because labeling schemes obscure the existence of certain documents pertinent to the researchers' inquiry. And in the course of all these activities, documents slip out of folders and get shoved into others, or somehow they find their way into pockets or briefcases. Thus, like the fountain, the archive is the sum total of all the actions undertaken by people who organize and service it as well as those who go searching through it. The memory archives produce is continually constructed and is neither permanent nor enduring nor authoritative.

Nowhere does this become more evident than in the project of "reconstructing a dance." Mique'l Dangeli (Tsimshian) describes the extensive protocols necessary to acquire access to a given dance within Northwest Coast Native communities: "Among Northwest Coast First Nations people, rights to songs, dances, and associated masks, headdresses, robes, and ceremonial regalia, are vehemently guarded as they are not only integral to individual and collective identity but they also define ownership of territories (both land and waterways)."[27] Ownership here refers to the custodial responsibilities of protecting Land as well as those ceremonies that celebrate connection to the Land. As in the act of obtaining knowledge from the archive, access to a dance requires considerable interaction and negotiation among multiple people and social groups. Memory is located partially in the actions themselves that eventually yield the proper conditions for performance of the dance.

How different is this from undertaking the reconstruction of a baroque opera or one of Vaslav Nijinsky's ballets?[28] On the one hand, there is seemingly easier access to librettos, musical and notated dance scores, iconographic materials documenting the dance, costume sketches, dimensions (and pitch in the case of baroque performances) of the stage, although they are stored in libraries that sometimes require letters of introduction from college presidents or the filling out of lengthy applications to gain access. On the other, people who reconstruct dances spend years acquiring the physical facility at dancing and the ability to read the notation that enable them to undertake a performance from the past, and these acts involve multiple kinds of interaction with others who have special skills and knowledge about how to transform notation into steps and movements or the sketch of a costume into a garment that can be worn.

The fact that these protocols need to be enacted in the process of reconstructing dance makes evident the extent to which reconstruction is actually re-creation. In the same way that cognitive scientists are demonstrating how autobiographical memory is newly constructed with each remembering, so, too, dances from the past are newly made in the present. Like De Brigard's thesis that remembering is a form of hypothetical or speculative thinking and the Western Apache practice of speaking with names, remembering consists of actions that simultaneously engage past and future. If, as one moves through the day, the memory that is distributed throughout the body is constantly updating, transforming, and recalibrating, then is remembering dancing a rehearsing of possibilities for how to move in the future as much as a reimagining of how one danced in the past?

Decolonizing Memory

Returning now to the question of whether the distinction between individual and social memory is a viable one, it is clear how the act of remembering a dance is infused with social engagement. Throughout the processes of learning to dance and learning a dance, the interactive and social dimensions are inseparable from individual recollection. Not only is memory not stored in the brain, it is continually re-created as the product of social encounters. Could part of the process of decolonizing memory entail calling into question the isolation of individual from social memory?

Certainly, the model of the archive as a hallowed collection of permanent documents representing the historical past needs to be revised, and along with that the concomitant assumption that an individual enters the archive and, on their own, finds the truth. Equally, the privileging of texts as superior to actions because they are more permanent should be questioned. Texts and images documenting past dances not only point to the impossibility of accurate and faithful remembering of a dance but also to the bias toward what the past is within the archive itself, in which texts are seen as more truthful than actions. By collecting only those traces of the past that endure for long periods of time, the traditional archive, and those who use it as such, fundamentally dismisses and disavows the significance of bodily movement in producing knowledge and the social connection through which it is generated.

A further violence to Native peoples has occurred through the collection of their artifacts and skeletal remains by museums, an alternative form of the archive. Dangeli explains that such unauthorized collection prevents the sacred exchange of spirit that would normally occur: "The interactions of creation, care, song, and dance that we have been trained to carry out in partnership with our Ceremonial Beings allow their lives to flourish. Their life is our ceremony. It is this symbiotic relationship that puts our world in balance. Our Ceremonial Beings need us to breathe life into them, just as we need them to breathe life into us."[29] Arguing that the spirit within these objects can never be owned by museums, she has created dances specifically for museum spaces that enact a connection to the Ceremonial Beings held there while also reminding visitors and staff of the wrongful collection of these materials.

As Dangeli's actions suggest, many Native and Indigenous conceptions of memory locate it not only in people, but also in other living beings, places and landscapes, and objects, including the bones of those who have left this life.[30] Memory issues not from within these various entities and beings but rather from the interfaces and interconnections among them. Memory within Native contexts often circulates through the telling of stories, as when Western Apache travel to places and tell stories about them, or when elders contribute thousands of place names to a map that Simpson constructs of the area around Toronto prior to the extensive urban development of the last hundred years. These place names document events that occurred and practices, such as hunting, fishing, gathering, or celebrating, that were a repeated part of living in reciprocal relation with the Land and its nonhuman inhabitants.[31]

The stories Native people share serve to consolidate and affirm tribal identity and underscore key values that members of the community share. For example, four distinctly different histories of the life of Sacagawea have been articulated by the Lemhi Shoshone, the Wind River Shoshone, the Comanche, and the Hidatsa. As Sally McBeth (settler-scholar) has shown, for each version of Sacagawea's life, she is claimed as a member of that tribe and as someone with certain talents and allegiances that enforce core commitments within the tribe. Among the Comanche, for example, several descendants are convinced she is their ancestor, whereas the historical records left by Meriwether Lewis (unmarked) and William Clark (unmarked) indicate that she was Shoshone. At the same time, there seems to be an understanding that the importance of the different versions of her life lies in their application to the present and future well-being of the community. As one Comanche tribal member put it, "I didn't say it was true, I said it was what I had heard."[32]

The intergenerational sharing of stories has been used not only to vivify the connection between event and place but also as an effective way to engage in what Simpson calls a "generative refusal of colonial recognition."[33] The ability to hold on to recollections of events over time has frequently served both to preserve Native knowledges and to prove injustice on the part of settler colonists.[34] As one example of this, Deborah Miranda (Esselen and Chumash) recounts the story of a young girl who was raped by a padre at the Carmel Mission in the early 1800s. Retaining that story by retelling it from one generation to the next for over one hundred years, her relative recited it to J. P. Harrington (unmarked), a Smithsonian ethnographer of Native life in California, in 1935. It was particularly important that the name of the victim, Vicenta Gutierrez, was remembered and passed on as a way to honor ancestors and provide "a charmstone of hope for future generations."[35] The strategic preservation and subsequent retelling of memories can destabilize the archive and repurpose it as part of a decolonial process.

Dance, as both a practice and subject of critical inquiry, makes evident the assumptions underlying the traditional conception of the archive as well as those envisioning the brain as a storehouse. As a form of knowledge production and transmission that is based in bodily movement, dance has long demonstrated the process of thinking as a form of moving. By continually proposing this equation of thinking and moving, dance, insofar as it is practiced within the Academy, with its courses in learning to dance and learning to make dances given academic credit, holds the potential to decolonize both the university and its archives.

Yet dance educators are also struggling to reorganize curricula that are rife with hierarchies of dances, singular definitions of technical excellence, and notions of more primitive and civilized dance genres. Courses in dance history absurdly trace the development of dance only from ancient Greece through the Renaissance, eighteenth and nineteenth centuries in Europe to the development of modern and postmodern dance in the US. Despite dance's potential to unsettle such a neat settler-colonial progression, such courses never even include an interrogation of what history is or how it is deployed to justify present and future actions. Pedagogies for teaching dancing, equally, rely on forms of instruction that identify a self that possesses a body and is capable of telling it what to do. Having gotten their foot in the door of the university, dance programs have often developed using the same Cartesian and colonial bedrock on which the Academy is based.

Intriguingly, one scholar whose teaching was very influential in the establishment of dance programs within the university is John Dewey (unmarked), an early proponent of the importance to cognition of sensorimotor connections. Dewey wrote an essay on the subject, "The Reflex Arc in Psychology," published in 1896, in which he argued against the notion of sensory stimulation as the origin of perception and instead privileged movement of the head, eyes, and body as determining the quality of what is experienced.[36] As a philosopher, educator, and public intellectual, Dewey instigated many educational reforms while on the faculties at the University of Chicago and Columbia University's Teachers College. A strong advocate for doing as a form of learning, Dewey's writings on education and curriculum development were cited frequently as justification for the inclusion of dance within the Academy. I have long been aware of Dewey's importance to dance education, but I think it is wonderful that I learned about his interest in sensorimotor pathways from a text on neuroscience published more than a century later. Don't you agree?

DANCING'S AFFORDANCES

Consider these instances of dancing: A dancer in a wheelchair careers onto the stage, executes a breathtaking wheelie and then exits. (It could be Black Briton and former AXIS Dance Company member Alice Sheppard, or UK-based Candoco Dance Company member Joel Brown, or New Zealand–based Suzanne Cowan.) Members of the all-white corps de ballet stand motionless for minutes providing "visual wallpaper" for the haunting duet between the prima ballerina and her princely partner.[1] (They could be performing on stages in Sydney, Moscow, Houston, or Seattle, among many other places.) Groups of mostly dark-skinned dancers, some seated, others crouched, form circles and stare intently at a solo dancer in the middle.[2] (They could have traveled from St. Louis, Boston, Salvador, or Manila to meet up in one of an equally diverse number of cities worldwide.) A solitary figure with a masklike face stands solemnly in front of a shagbark hickory, her arms extended sideward serving as shelves for handwritten volumes of books, all carefully titled except for a few whose spines remain blank. Her name is Meryl McMaster, and she is Canadian and Plains Cree.

What does dancing afford the wheelchair dancer? A complete absorption in the action along with a sense of fitting perfectly into the dance as it is unfolding, and subsequent satisfaction in having pulled it off at just the right moment in the ongoing action? And what about the dancers representing a flock of swans standing quietly in a semicircle? The increasing fatigue of the raised arm, the boredom and resentment of being used as decoration along with a sense of purpose and conviction? How about the sweaty dancers in the cypher channeling the communal energy of the crew while riding high on the incredible inventiveness of the soloist in the middle? Or the Native performer standing vigilantly in the pale winter light, registering the weight of so much knowledge and her responsibility in supporting it? (The title of her piece is *Time's Gravity*.)

These scenarios of dancing, all from recent times, summon up histories of domination and subordination as well as control over versus immersion within the fact of dancing. In so doing, they push back against the simplistic assumption that dancing makes people happy. What else might dancing do within or beyond these strongly contrasting moments of dancing? What might it afford? Gibson, who developed the concept of affordances in the 1970s, has been highly influential in fields ranging from urban planning to architecture and design, yet his pertinence to the study of dance has rarely been considered. What might a theory of perception based in the centrality of moving have to say about what dancing is and does? Examining dancing through the lens of affordances, I will move first into a consideration of certain kinds of disability, where I hope to highlight how dancing enables an awareness of bodily presence as always fusing with its particular surroundings. Subsequently, I will consider how learning to dance can not only construct a specific kind of body but also orient body to world in distinct ways. Finally, I will consider more broadly what dancing affords, both individually and collectively. Throughout, I will continue to transplant myself into foreign situations and endeavor to feel what kinds of knowing moving yields.

Dancing's Niches

As I have discussed throughout this volume, the entire body, interconnected as it is with its surroundings, perceives the world by moving. Walking up the fire road, and considering for the moment only what I see, I notice the changing edges of rocks, grasses, and bushes as they progressively obscure or make evident what lies behind them. I also notice my arms protruding into and out of my visual field, and if I look down, my legs and feet. As they move, there is a deletion of optical information at their leading edge and an accretion at the trailing edge.[3] This, along with varying pressures on the bottoms of my feet, the exertion of leg muscles, the transient whiffs of sage or eucalyptus and the feel of breeze on my cheeks, is how I come to know the body as an entity moving through and among other things and beings. The deletion and accretion of surfaces is also how I know that things are there even when not seen. I experience the rock I have just walked past as existing even when it is no longer in my field of vision. Its surfaces have progressively covered the grasses behind it while also revealing new facets of itself.

A rock also knows its world—the heat from the sun, the dampness of the fog, the small plant that is pushing through the earth right next to it. The rock and I partially share a niche. There are places it cannot go that I can know as I move into them, and it understands a kind of solidity and quietude that I do not because our physicalities are so different.[4] At the same time, our shared and individual niches change over time, as the land becomes hotter and more arid, and my joints get more arthritic.

For many people termed "disabled," the organism-environment interfaces are simply different, rendering them differently abled. Their capacities for integrating visual, aural, and haptic sensations with proprioceptive and vestibular information concerning the status of the body may be different, leading to the perception of different sets of affordances. Locomoting through the world in a motorized wheelchair, for example, affords quick changes in the speed at which one moves, but not the opportunity to change levels to scrutinize one's surroundings. Stairs do not afford climbing, but hills with smooth surfaces can easily be mounted. A focus on the connectedness of all things, and in particular, the interface between body and world, prompts a reenvisioning of how people engage with their niche and the many creative options they enact for perceiving, locomoting, and obtaining information from that environment.

As illustration of this, Vivian Sobchack (California-based settler-scholar), whose leg was amputated above the knee, describes her experience with crutches this way: "If one learns how to use crutches properly, they are extraordinarily liberating. Indeed, one can move more quickly and with greater exuberance on crutches than on one's own two legs (whether prosthetic or not). The span of one's gait increases and there is a cadenced and graceful 'swing through' effect that not only covers ground but also propels the lived body forward in pleasingly groundless ways not allowed by mere walking. There is, both phenomenologically and empirically, a 'lift' to one's step."[5] Sobchack is comparing her experience of crutches with the more effortful labor of learning to walk with a prosthetic leg assisted by a cane. Managing the new leg requires a completely new sequencing of the activation of abdominal, pelvic, and leg muscles, yet as she observes, the experience of walking with crutches, although also requiring practice, offers an exuberance that walking without them does not produce.

Dancing's Affordances · 99

Similarly, dancer Homer Avila (Hispanic), who lost a leg and hip to cancer, approaches his transformed body as a "new morphology," exploring what new affordances it creates.[6] As he explains: "I do not stand in front of you with the mind-set that I am not a two-legged dancer.... It's not about looking at an aspect of partial function. What you are seeing is the wholeness of this organism. And what impresses me most about this organism—this corpus—is that you may alter it in so many ways, and still it has this incredible desire to have an expression of life."[7] Avila straightforwardly challenges the ableist assumption that a nonnormative physicality is inherently deficient. He points instead to the resilience, even eagerness, of the body to engage with its surroundings and express itself.

Sobchack and Avila each experienced a different kind of alteration to their niche that required different kinds of accommodations to move in the world. As referenced earlier in this volume, the niches that humans inhabit are partially formed through the cultural values of the society in which they live and include social, political, aesthetic, sexual, fighting, and cooperative forms of engagement, among others.[8] The niches that humans build also include markers of identity such as gender, race, class, and ability, which help define how people circulate through their environments and what is available to them. Resisting any distinction between what are "natural" and "cultural" features, the niches that Sobchack and Avila came to construct contain not only new ways of getting around but also encounters with people who undoubtedly hold different prejudices about disability that yield encounters based in solicitous care and respect but also disgust and disregard.

Pursuing an inquiry into these kinds of interactions, Arseli Dokumaci (Canada-based settler-scholar) shows how people also function as affordances, particularly in situations where someone needs assistance to negotiate various features in the environment. They also provide affordances for one another by not interacting in certain ways, such as when they refrain from touching someone for whom touch is painful.[9] She further argues that people can sometimes actively interfere with a potential affordance, as when they do not make a place for a wheelchair user to get on the bus.[10] Expanding on these observations, Brian Bell (United States–based settler-scholar) and Jennifer Clegg (Texas-based settler-scholar) advocate for the ways that affordances could be used to develop and guide institutional policy decisions that benefit the experiencing of affordances by those who are variously disabled.[11]

Extending this kind of argument much further, Julie Minich (Texas-based settler-scholar) and Jina Kim (Asian American) argue that within neoliberal societies, the emphasis on the individual and on the body as one's personal property creates a condition in which peoples' health appears to be a personal choice rather than an unevenly distributed access to care. They recommend implementing a reorientation of disability studies away from a focus on specific objects of study and toward the processes through which disability is constructed. Kim proposes a "crip-of-color critique" in which the habitus itself constructs precarious populations through the unequal distribution of resources. Focusing in particular on race-based forms of discrimination, she urges a consideration of "the ways in which the state, rather than protecting disabled people, in fact operates as an apparatus of racialized disablement, whether through criminalization and police brutality, or compromised public educational systems and welfare reform."[12] Kim points to an ableist epistemology that dovetails with racialized forms of discrimination to levy accusations of "insanity, criminality, stupidity, or dependency" when, in fact, they have been insufficiently supported.[13] Minich adds to this the importance of considering all forms of discrimination, including transmisia, heteropatriarchy, colonialism, and capitalist exploitation. All these prejudicial structures and processes within neoliberal societies are part of the affordances in which people are variously immersed.

Lavonna Lovern (Georgia-based settler-scholar) and others have pointed out that the categorization of certain people as "disabled" reflects a colonialist perspective, one that presumes the isolated autonomy of the individual and ascribes to that individual the capacity to succeed or fail. As a consequence, disability is figured as the individual's responsibility.[14] In contrast, many Native orientations toward difference acknowledge all peoples' varying capacities to give whatever is needed to support the community while also doing no harm. Within this orientation, difference is accepted as an inevitable part of what humanness is. As Lovern explains: "Indeed, many traditional Indigenous languages have no word for 'disabled' or 'handicapped.' Moreover as all beings exhibit differences, there is no preferential position designated as 'normal' or 'ideal.' Neither do these communities establish a negative dichotomous position based on difference."[15] Instead of disability, Lovern proposes that individuals embody diverse talents, all of which can make a vital contribution to the balance of the community. It is each member's responsibility to ensure that everyone gets the assistance they need to contribute their talent.[16] As Avila also insists, each and every body has the desire to express itself.

So, what can a consideration of Sobchack's and Avila's situations reveal about dancing? Dancing takes place within and as part of the various niches that humans inhabit. It can expand or reinforce affordances established throughout this habitus. It can, for example, reiterate social codes for gendered comportment, or affirm an aesthetic preference for asymmetry, or confirm connections to a spirit world, or offer a "great" evening. Or it could probably afford all of these at once. Through the rhythmic patterns it establishes within the body, the proximities to others it invites, the ways it directs and focuses attention, the senses of fatigue and excitement it incites, dancing constructs familiar and foreign states of being. Following Young's notion of throwability, what dancing affords also depends on what people have learned to rely on it for—as a conduit for cultural memory, a form of social play, a way of feeling alive. Dancing takes people beyond, or back, or into, concocting complex and multilayered experiences of the body, memory, and sociality.

Humans often start dancing as young children, frequently in response to seeing others dancing. Yet, dancing also seems to erupt in young bodies as a form of spontaneous exploration of what a body can do. Wiggling, twisting, jumping, and shimmying all produce distinct sensations in the musculature and joints that coordinate with visual, haptic, and vestibular information to produce novel effects. Children explore these coordinated effects as a way to better understand their world and how they can move within it. They spontaneously try out new moves, jumping excitedly, swaying repeatedly, turning endlessly, or accenting particular parts of the body simply to feel what action does.

Children are also taught how to dance by others, a process that stipulates certain movement patterns, specific ways to interact with others and with music, and particular and more general meanings and values that the act of dancing brings forth. They learn how to be cool, graceful, funky, sexy, stylish, manly, sincere, or proper through a particular angling of the elbows, a sideways glance of the eyeballs, a swirl of the pelvis, a lifting or grounding of bodily force, and myriad other patternings of movement. They might also learn to avoid dancing, finding in its coordinated sequences an overwhelming discomfort and consequent sense of clumsiness or inadequacy. Sobchack, for example, writes about the compulsory ballroom dance classes that she took as a teenager. The necessity of matching movement to musical beat or rhythm seemed impossible, leading to feelings of embarrassment.[17] Dancing with a partner might also feel uncomfortably strange. The coerced cooperation with a partner might even be experienced as repugnant. Standards for beauty, grace, stylishness, attractiveness, or endurance could easily seem unattainable, prompting people to hide or move away from dancing whenever it occurs.

To varying degrees, people learn dancing by watching and copying others' dancing, or they listen to someone describing movement, and they sometimes receive encouragement or correction delivered verbally or through touch. Repeating these movements, they also experiment with how to refine them to adapt them specifically to their physicality. Dancing to music, dancing with others, dancing in particular places—all elicit further refinements and alterations to movement that establish habits of moving within the body. Dancing thereby supplements and also influences the larger habitualized repertoire of motions in which the body participates.

The niches of humans transform over time. As observed previously, what an eighteen-year-old body can do is markedly different from the capacities of an eighty-year-old body, and these differences alter the niche, both in its size and options for certain kinds of interactions. Events that bodies experience mark them, sometimes deeply, causing some ways of moving to disappear or become more pronounced. Trauma, injury, chronic tension, or persistent fear can all alter the niche, just as happiness, contentment, and a sense of security can remake what seems possible.

Thus, as I envision it, after centuries of discrimination and exclusion, disabled dancers emblazon themselves on the stage, proclaiming new possibilities for how, when, and where to move. Among these possibilities are the myriad ways of tuning body to chair. As Wheelchair Dancer (the pseudonym sometimes used by Alice Sheppard) explains, "Modern dance activates my chair. I get in it, out of it, partner it, lift it, wheelie it, spin it, lie on it, hang on it, balance my partner on it, slop out of it, push with it, dismantle it."[18] Thus dancing can afford an experience of body and chair in their intensifying fusion. In strong contrast, the corps de ballet dancer's utter dedication to her art steadies her arms, as with each musical phrase she is reminded of the need to remain quiet and lovely to look at. Does dancing on this stage deepen her commitment to the ensemble and its role in portraying a beautiful if tragic story? What about the dancers breaking in the battle? Do they feel the resistive and triumphant power of the Africanist diasporic aesthetic values transforming into a global language of uplift and empowerment after centuries of denigration?[19] Does dancing fuse music, movement, and spirit for them as they utilize competition with themselves and others to fuel the energy and connection within the cypher, affording an even more powerful sense of community? Emerging differently from centuries of colonization and endangerment, McMaster, communing with the sturdy tree behind her, carries Indigenous knowledge from the past and also, because some of the volumes have yet to be written or titled, the promise of a resilient future. Does this moment of performance, requiring so much strength and stillness, afford a commemoration of the power and vitality that unites all beings? In each of these cases, what dancing does is throw awareness onto the connectedness or alienation that is continually emerging.

Just as the niche changes over a lifetime, dancing also changes. Consider, for example, the contrasts in popular dances in the US over the twentieth century—from the waltz and polka to the Charleston and Lindy Hop, through the twist and into disco and hip-hop. Each of these forms affords different kinds of interaction between partners and within a group dancing together. Each stipulates different gender roles encoded in its postures and gestures, the proximities of bodies to one another, the parts of the body that are featured, and who initiates what kind of movement. These values within the dance movement itself reverberate throughout the habitus, often reinforcing normative proscriptions for behavior, but sometimes suggesting new approaches to being in the world. The Lindy Hop, for example, modeled how two people could improvise individually and then resume a movement phrase in unison, the twist introduced new mores around the bodily display of sexually charged parts of the body, and hip-hop sourced gravity in a new way to proclaim a defiant resistance against pervasive neoliberal corruption.[20] Dancing affords all these things while alerting people to the fact that how they are moving changes what they perceive and hence what they know.

Dancing Colonially and Decolonially

Unlike baseball players who do not measure the arc of the ball they are running to catch but instead learn to move to the place where they can no longer see it accelerating toward them, dancers may or may not learn to measure the distance between each other in inches or feet just as they may also learn to count steps and measure time in seconds and minutes. They learn through various pedagogical projects to command the body or, alternatively, to locate control in the interface between body and surroundings.

In my walk up the fire road, for instance, I can choose to time my ascent, striving each day for a quicker climb that would prove my increasing fitness in terms of leg strength and aerobic capacity. Within this framework, a measuring mind commands respiratory and muscular systems to push ahead, knowing that as the body becomes more winded and fatigued, its stress at breathing and stepping will lead to greater capacity in a few days. I can just as well head up the road, focused on how the world is unfolding with each step. Each motion of the leg yields new information about my surroundings, and, like the baseball player's quick sprint, the control over next actions is located in the interface between me and what is around me. Experiencing this connectedness, I wink at the rock. Does the rock reciprocate by tripping me ever so slightly as my foot brushes across its surface?

Explicating further this notion of control within rather than command over, Wheelchair Dancer describes her relationships with her wheels in which wheeler and wheels fuse in the act of the push and together they explore and obtain information from their surroundings. She explains it this way: "When I push, I feel the force ride up through my body as my shoulders push down and out. It's a move of power, yes, but it is also a move that looks for the momentum of the chair. *I* emerge from the push. It's a move that suggests a butterfly coming out of its chrysalis; instead, my body picks up the forward movement and together we ride the power out into the world."[21] Clearly identifying how her own sense of identity emerges from the interface between body and chair, Dancer also imbues the chair with the kind of vitality that Bennett ascribes to all matter.[22] Citing Bennett, Julia Watts Belser (Washington, DC–based settler-scholar) locates Dancer and wheels as part of a larger and complex system of matter.[23] Having connected with what the chair affords, Dancer and chair then launch forward, discovering what bumps or cracks in the ground there might be, its slope and texture, along with the sights and sounds detected through the forward motion. Furthermore, as Watts Belser makes clear, Dancer's body is not deficient but rather empowered by a technology that extends and expands it.[24]

Because the entire body, including its prosthetic extensions, whether wheels, sticks, or cochlear implants, perceives the world, it comes to know the world. Applying an ecological cognitive science perspective, knowing is not only distributed across the whole body, it is an extension of perceiving.[25] For those using wheelchairs, knowing spreads to the chair itself in that different chairs are built with different capacities and sensitivities based on the materials used and their construction.[26] Different kinds of knowing also issue from wheelchairs that are self-pushed, pushed by others, or electrically powered. When the wheelchair is pushed by another person, that person enters into the bond between wheeler and chair as an additional interface with the world, producing, for example, sustained or lurching motion and quick or slow speeds.[27] All these ways of moving generate different perceptual experiences and an awareness of the continual connectedness with the flux of all that is around one.

Many dance pedagogies, particularly those in the Eurocentric concert dance tradition, strongly counter or deny this fusedness of body and surroundings. Growing out of an understanding of the body as both isolable and moldable, they approach the body as responsive to instruction. Indeed, the entire Western canon of dance manuals lays out the attributes of proper dancing and how to teach dances by emphasizing the individual shaping and timing of the body's movement. The earliest of these manuals, Domenico da Piacenza's (unmarked) *De arte saltandi et choreas ducendi*, published sometime in the 1450s or '60s, along with Antonio Cornazzano's (unmarked) *Libro dell'arte del danzare* (1455) and Guglielmo Ebreo da Pesaro's (unmarked) *De pratica seu arte tripudii* (1463), explain specific steps, qualities of movement, proper manners and comportment, and knowledge of musical forms on which the dances are rhythmically based. Not yet a kind of machine composed of muscles, sinews, and bones that is commanded by a mind (that comes with the invention of the turn-out machine in the eighteenth century), the body is nonetheless identified as capable of taking instruction. While there are notable differences in the pedagogical methods in these manuals as well as the circumstances of their authors, it is worth noting that they all slightly predate Columbus's voyage west.[28] Is the epistemic foundation for conquest also being laid during the dance lessons at the northern Italian courts?[29]

Today's training regimens, by contrast, push the body much harder. Students of different genres of dance, each with their own criteria for aesthetic perfection, frequently pursue competence and excellence by commanding the body, willing and even forcing it to extend further, higher, longer, and faster. Often with the help of a mirror through which dancers scrutinize their own appearance, learning to dance becomes a process of reconciling felt muscular effort with the visual appearance of the body reflected in the mirror or the observations and corrections of the teacher. In this approach to training, dancers aspire to deliver movement as product, one that meets both aesthetic and physical criteria of excellence. The body's performance is measured in terms of speed, height, number, and degree. The metrics, based in a visual assessment of the body in space, matter.

Perhaps the appeal of this approach stems from the body's capacity to increase its strength, flexibility, and endurance. Bodies do respond and improve performance as a result of the activities in which they engage. The field of dance science, an offshoot of sports science, has developed precisely to investigate and enhance the body's "fitness" for dancing and to improve its capabilities. Analyzing what is required to perform specific actions such as turning or jumping, it offers procedures of assessment as well as programs for expanding, in the most efficient way, muscular strength and flexibility, aerobic capacity, and dexterity. Dance science also addresses the suitability of the body to perform and the likeliness of injury, based on alignment, muscular imbalances, weakness, and sometimes bodily proportions. This breaking down of the body into constituent parts and capacities conceives of the body as matter on which a will can be applied to produce a movement. The mind copies and stores movement patterns and then tells the body what to do.

The instructions dance teachers give to students working in these traditions reinforce this conception of a mindless body first by divorcing mind from self. The simple directive "Place your arm here" builds on three interrelated assumptions: first, that there is a command central from which orders are issued to the arm; second, that there is a self that owns the arm (and the rest of the body) as a form of property; and third, that a spatial location can be established through calculating and then replicating a given shape. The directive further assumes that an unimpeded connection exists between seeing eyes, a processing brain, and muscular responses, and in many pedagogies this assumption underlies the conversion of sensations of momentum, balance, torque, contact, and tension across the surface and within the body into geometrized positions and trajectories. Rather than the moving through, they emphasize a singular position and then the next.

Even the spaces in which training takes place underscore the experience of the body as shapable matter. When held in rectangular rooms, with smooth, uncluttered floors and blank walls, classes emphasize the body's placement within a geometric configuration whose coordinates it will assimilate. This seemingly barren space directs attention onto the imprint and impact the body can make on it, promising fulfillment through the act of impressing oneself into it. Sometimes exercises entail dancing with others, but most often individual bodies perform spaced evenly apart from one another in rows that reinforce a geometric perception of the room.

Often, such pedagogies proceed incrementally through months and years of practice, with each phase of training augmenting competency through proven techniques for expanding bodily skills. Specific movements, designed to serve as the underlying support for more complex motions, are repeated daily, slowly molding flesh into a targeted set of abilities that support the execution of more complex sequences. Graded in terms of difficulty based on their visual and rhythmic clarity, these sequences serve as the metrics through which teachers sort and rank students, awarding to each of them distinctive achievements and deficiencies. Students, in turn, assimilate such assessments of themselves, continually objectifying their bodies and, equally, prioritizing the kinds of motion that produce the desired look in each moment. Rather than noticing the diverse forms of information that moving produces, they zero in on how it can produce specific visual designs. Rather than extend an invitation to all types of bodies to participate, these techniques shun the opportunity to provide accommodations for differing abilities and bodily shapes.

Students build up their capacity to parse space and, equally, the ability to assess themselves by applying various forms of measurement along with desired aesthetic principles. They feel the elation that comes from a momentary achievement and the satisfaction of sensing their expanding competence. They also experience frustration and disappointment as they internalize the shouted encouragements, barked orders, and withering sarcasm directed at them. Again, these instructions assume that excellence itself is measurable and, consequently, that students can be compared with one another and, often, placed in competition. Having repeated exercises so many times and worked so hard to improve, students make over the body into something that succeeds or fails, often registering for years afterward residual feelings of anxiety or inadequacy.

Other dance pedagogies focus on the person rather than the body, asking students to bring attention to or activate intelligence within a given part or region of the body. "Allow the sternum to lift" ascribes capacity and agency to the sternum and eliminates ownership, even though it implies that something is doing the allowing. Instead of focusing on the acquisition of specific skills, these pedagogies encourage students to expand awareness of proprioceptive sensation, gravitational pull, and bodily momentum. Less concerned with achieving a specific shape and delivering the body into that shape at a given time, they ask students to engage actively in tuning in to the information continually provided by the body itself—what moving in a certain way feels like. Some approaches utilize metaphors in which the body is likened to other events in the natural world. Others focus on coordinating proprioceptive sensation and anatomical potential, so that students gain a deeper understanding of how one can move. Bodies with different capacities are invited into these practices as people whose intelligences can contribute to the group's understanding of their collective identity and of what humanness is more generally.[30]

But what about using a directive such as "The sternum lifts" instead of "Allow the sternum to lift"? What if the body becomes parts or places or actions that simply occur? Is this the direction in which decolonial dance learning could or should move? The use of the possessive implies ownership over, on the one hand, and it asserts agency, on the other. What if prompts are suggested in a soft, gentle voice or with spirited enthusiasm? Since these directives eventually transform into what the body is and how it is experienced, it is important to consider who does what, who is losing or gaining, mustering fortitude or relinquishing with relief. I have no answers for these questions except to suggest that various pedagogies be tried, and their results tracked and reflected on over time.

Some pedagogies combine aspects of each of these approaches. They might alternate between attending to how movement feels and counting a length of time. They could focus on analyzing the rhythmic complexity of the musical accompaniment and encourage many possible kinds of steps that could be made in response but then add instructions concerning the angle of the head or the carriage of the arms. Students could be directed to explore the moving point of contact between two bodies as they share weight, and then asked to conclude that exploration within a given number of counts. Dancers could also be taught a very specific phrase of movement but then be asked to experiment with varying it and otherwise expanding on it. It is not that the prompts to lengthen, lift, stretch, or firm are always forms of bodily colonization, however it is worth considering what happens when they are implemented to achieve a desired product rather than as a process of tuning in to bodily intelligence.

Of course, many people learn to dance simply by dancing alongside others and copying or otherwise interpreting their movements. The Caribbean, Brazilian, and Native dancers described earlier in this volume all learned dancing in this way. Perhaps they were guided with touch or a few instructions, but often, dancers learn primarily through doing. Inspired by moving in synchrony with others and by the opportunity to focus on the act of moving itself, they twist, bend, stomp, arch, contract, extend, shake, and roll, sometimes incorporating gestures or styles from family and friends, and in this way, they can continue to dance with these people when they are no longer near. Still other dancers invite spirits or ancestors to dance them, opening themselves to other beings who move them in unique ways.

Whatever the form of dance training, it profoundly remakes not just the body but also the person. Learning to dance through any of these methods, dancers absorb not only the physical movements themselves but also the many meanings and values they embody. The act of dancing creates an entire world of meaning. Sometimes assigned to the movement as part of a social or aesthetic contract, as in the mudras of Bharatanatyam or the motions of pantomime, these meanings are much more often built into physical action as an intrinsic aspect of moving. Actions as simple as looking upward, surging forward, or turning from side to side, for example, carry with them connotations regarding one's sense of being in the world, and even the nature of that world. These are further reinforced as people dance with and alongside one another.

Turning from how dance is learned to how it is studied, it is worth noting the coloniality of the categories that have been used within the Western canon to classify dance. Are the traditional distinctions between concert dance, social dance, and ceremonial dance, for example, really justifiable? In each, a group of people convenes to move together while others gather to watch, and in each, values are expressed through the choreographic organization of peoples' locations in relation to one another along with the movements they perform and their sequencing. Each event is seen as special and efficacious, with its participants coordinating actions collectively, and in each, dancing affords discovery—possibles of possibility: possibles that include communing, suffering, enduring, delighting, achieving, resisting, remembering, seducing, competing, worshipping, awakening, and more.

Often, the efforts to distinguish between types of dancing and assign them different functions reveal attempts to instantiate hierarchies of value. The assumption that communitarian forms of dancing and dance-making develop out of "primitive" motivations whereas concert stage performances reflect the higher mental functions of abstraction and symbolization can be seen as based in Cartesian assumptions about what the mind is and how it works. The assertion that some forms of dancing are more refined because they are more "abstract" becomes untenable. Decolonial theories of perception and mind, in contrast, suggest that all forms of dancing engage in processes of perceiving and responding to others and the environment, thereby constructing worlds within it.

Affordances also provide for a reevaluation of disability, and conceptions of the body as machine more generally. They give insight into how humans grow and age, and how different organisms' niches are interconnected. Considering what the world affords one disorders the systems of categorization generated from an omniscient and singular viewpoint that so effectively rationalized colonization. A focus on affordances reorders the world according to the specific capacities and limitations of a given organism within its niche. The theory of affordances encourages a rethinking of the assumption that individuals are separate from their surroundings, rather than interfaced with them through the relations and forms of engagement that are perceived.

What Dancing Affords

Although affordances are the content of experience, replete with values and meanings, people rarely perceive affordances themselves. Rather, people perceive the world that they make available to them, and they perceive ways of acting in that world. As mentioned earlier, in moving through the day, little attention is paid to physical actions unless they fail to produce the desired effects. I grab something off the shelf, open a door, drink a glass of water. Yet in accomplishing these tasks, I tend not to notice the grasping action or the maneuvering forward and back to reach and then open the door, or the actions involved in balancing a full glass.

To illustrate this point, Chemero analyzes the simple act of standing in a line. To maintain one's balance and the appropriate distance behind the person standing in front, he suggests:

> Try to direct your attention to how things look and feel as you stand there, swaying gently and adjusting the felt pressures on different parts of your feet. You will notice these felt changes to the pressures—accomplished by flexing and relaxing the muscles of your feet, legs, and torso—come along with the slight optical expansion and contraction of the hairs on the back of the head of the person in front of you in line.

You are seeing that person's head move slightly closer and then slightly farther away, which is seeing both that you are falling toward (or away from) the person and the affordance for leaning backward (or forward) slightly to keep your body upright by applying pressure with different parts of your feet.[31]

Chemero's point in offering this description is that what the floor, gravity, and proprioceptive, visual, and vestibular systems, acting in concert with the musculature, afford is the act of maintaining balance while standing in place. Actions such as these continually enable one's experience of the world.

As Chemero emphasizes, people seldom notice affordances themselves, and yet, when dancing, it is precisely these relations that often become the focus of attention. Yes, one notices one's surroundings—the people, sounds or music, objects, décor, etc. in the milieu—but one also attends far more acutely to how one is moving and to the effects that moving produces. Dancing affords an experiencing of affordances similar to Chemero's suggestion to direct attention to the act of standing in a line behind someone. Because movement itself becomes the content of the experience, it focuses attention precisely on how physical motion alters perception, how it alters gravity's pull, and how it demands a recalibration of balance. It reveals how one is interfaced with and perceives the world.

Crucially, what the act of dancing affords is the experience of physicality itself as well as the consequences of any movement. The wheelchair and corps de ballet dancers, for example, are not imagining themselves as able-bodied dancers or the prima ballerina. The wheelchair dancers are not triumphing over their disability; they are, I imagine, as Avila explains, expressing the physicality that they are. The corps de ballet dancers, aware of their contribution to the ensemble and the spectacle it is presenting, most likely experience their fatigue as proof of their commitment. The dancers breaking and McMaster, each knowing a different history of extreme marginalization, sense in their exertions the power of proclaiming a vibrant existence. The breaking dancers pulled into the cypher's energy sometimes connect with ancestors and lost loved ones, experiencing a euphoric in-the-moment timelessness that heals and makes more space for community.[32] McMaster, having carefully chosen the tree, her clothing, and face paint, as well as fabricating the books she will carry, assembles it all, and with a grace that is both pragmatic and ceremonial, composes herself for the photograph that will carry her forward in time, disseminating an image of Native practices that she, rather than any colonial observers of her people, has composed.

Learning to dance (like practicing yoga or training for a sport), one is introduced to the possibility of noticing both how moving alters perception and what the resulting effect of moving is. Regardless of pedagogical approach, when teachers ask students to expand a surface of the body or grip a particular set of muscles, the results of these actions are assessed relative to one's previous posture and also to one's new relations with the world. Some sets of actions produce a higher jump; others yield a smoother transition; still others keep the movement on the beat. Actions open into other actions, all of which are noticed in a way that differs from daily life, wherein movement is most often a means to some end other than the experiencing of the movement itself.

From infancy one becomes accustomed to certain relations between, for example, what one sees as a hand moves toward the face while the cupboard door is opening, but these habitualized relations are altered during dancing such that novel experiences of the connection between the action of perception and the action of moving parts of the body come into being. Dancing actualizes new forms of the flow and nonflow (or rest) of visual, aural, haptic, and proprioceptive sensations, and it equally makes manifest singular and sometimes surprising sensations of the distribution of weight across the body as well as the need to breathe more rapidly or slow down and rest.

Through this recalibration of awareness, dancing affords an intense focus on the immediacy of knowing, in the sense that, as Gibson argues, what is known is what is experienced. This knowing is also exceedingly transient, as the body passes from one place-time to the next, an experience that the act of dancing emphasizes. In this sense, dancing intensifies the nowness of living. In its evanescence, dancing also offers a continual emerging into the next and the new. Much has been made of dancing's ephemerality and the fact that it vanishes immediately. Some have championed its traceless intangibility, while others have decried its inability to develop permanence.[33] What dancing affords certainly includes this experience of transientness, but it is important to distinguish its impermanence from the focus that dancing throws onto nowness. Although it is possible to dance distractedly, the fact of moving continually resets attention on the now. This happens most emphatically when the dancer is improvising the movement, but it also occurs during the performance of routine and habitualized actions. Dancing continually grabs and focuses attention on itself.

As Avila makes clear, the experience of dancing is also perpetually one of creation and discovery. Performing a movement, even one that has been repeatedly practiced to the point of rote execution, comes with an awareness of the body's emergence in the world. Each stretch, bend, burst, twist, lunge, and lift comes with changes in bodily shape, affording the perception of new surfaces and new sensations of gravity's pull, all coordinated with the transforming proprioceptive information registered in muscles, ligaments, and tendons. A different part of the foot suddenly senses more weight bearing down through it; one leg brushes past the other affording a brief sensation of touch; the vestibular system registers the momentum of a whirl, one that also brings a momentary scent that just as suddenly evaporates. In all these ways, dancing directs attention to bodily action and the sensations it produces. As such, dancing affords the experience of change. It focuses awareness on that change and on what is becoming known in each instant.

Often, people with different kinds of abilities have a similar experience as they navigate their surroundings. The failures of the built environment to provide access call attention to the interface between how one is moving and what it yields. Alternatively, the successes in mobility, decipherability, and other kinds of engagement with the world also focus attention on affordances themselves. As Sobchack observes:

> Through the course of a single day, my mode and experience of movement shifts and changes. As is the case with anyone else, this is, in part, because, through the course of a day, I inhabit different kinds of space (both safe and perilous) and engage in myriad different tasks and projects (both familiar and strange). However, more singularly, these shifts in my modes of bodily movement tend to be more varied, occur more frequently, and occupy my self consciousness more often than is the case with most people. This is because, over a relatively short period of time, I am variously one-legged, two-legged, and three-legged (as well as, in my car, four-wheeled). Each of these incarnations involves its own bodily rhythm, speed, and "protocol." . . . In a certain sense, then, I am not so far removed from the self-consciousness and bodily calculation that occupy athletes and dancers—if perhaps not in performance, then surely in preparation.[34]

Where Chemero asks readers to direct their attention to the act of standing in line, Sobchack's daily experience of moving through the world inherently focuses her on how she is accomplishing it, a process that she suggests is similar to the act of dancing.

Dancing affords all these experiences both individually and collectively when people, never isolated from others, create worlds together as they dance. As Anderson argues, humans move in order to achieve certain effects in and on the world, and expanding on this idea, he proposes that language, or more precisely, the active practice of speaking or what he calls "languaging," affords opportunities to achieve a variety of results.[35] He suggests that it is through speaking that humans achieve specific effects, get certain things to happen, and, sometimes, gain control over situations. Speaking affords the objectification of entities and events. It also augments memory, and crucially, it affords social coordination that produces relations of power.

Dancing similarly affords all these opportunities, palpably manifesting the exercise of power. The wheelchair dancer is helping to forge a new genre, that of mixed-ability dance, that fundamentally challenges viewers' expectations concerning the dancing they will see. The corps de ballet dancer, participating in a form that has long proclaimed its preeminence as both an art and approach to training the body, steadfastly holds to all she has achieved as a dancer whose expertise merits inclusion. As the dance crews who compete in battles travel in order to participate internationally, exchanging styles and practices, they exhilarate in the global popularity of an Africanist diasporic form whose defiantly nonerect kinestheme offers sustenance to dancers undergoing multiple forms of marginalization.[36] McMaster creates her performances to be photographed so that they circulate to galleries and museums and live an impactful life online while also blurring boundaries between visual art and performance.[37] In each case, dancing affords knowing the complexity of meanings layered into each moment of moving and the differing investments of all those involved.

Dancing can take people places, engaging them in the common project of togetherness. It can enable dancers to come into unison with one another, creating solidarity, and also construct extensions of or reactions to one another's movement, as a kind of conversation. Likewise, dancing affords various experiences of touch and of weight sharing. During dancing, one can practice control and coordination of the body by oneself and with others. And these shared experiences evolve over the time spent dancing.

This togetherness can manifest as an egalitarian back-and-forth, a partnership with distinct roles for each dancer, or as a connection marked by degrees of domination and subjection. Square dances, ballroom dances, break dances, mixed-ability dances—each configures the relations among members of the group distinctively, ordaining specific distributions of power through the spatial organization of dancers and their actions with and toward one another.

The square, for example, that partners construct affirms the egalitarian cooperation of all four pairs of dancers and the special connection that members of the duo have to each other, but the choreography also emphasizes the individuality of each dancer as they engage with those across the corners and form circles of braided locomotion. Ballroom dancing centers much more on the individual duo and the division of labor between the partners as one leads and the other follows, making their way around the dance floor. Break dances use the circular spatial formation to support a conversation in which each dancer's solo includes a response to the dancing that preceded it, eventually incorporating the contributions of all members of the group. Mixed-ability companies of dancers coordinate forms of action available to their members, often creating complex interdependencies within the group.

Sighted people watching dancing become similarly engaged in their own proprioceptive systems. As the research on mirror neurons has shown, seeing a movement activates the same neuromuscular patterns as those that are performing that movement.[38] Listening to someone describe dancing may also elicit similar kinesthetic responses. Watching dancers perform feats unattainable by viewers nonetheless takes those viewers on a journey. Watching differently abled dancers perform with one another may expand viewers' awareness of the potential to explore different sets of affordances and asks them to infer how people might perceive differently. Such performances also elucidate the ways in which dancers who are differently abled operate within niches that are partially shared and overlapping.

As dancers inhabit these forms of connection, they are often able to proclaim or even insist on something important about who they are. Or they can try out new identities or even transform into other people or beings. Performing these identities, for or alongside others, stretches the shared niche, adding new possibilities for how to be in relation with each other and with one's surroundings, including more-than-human entities and beings. At Carnival, Gay Pride, Turtle Dances, Vodun ceremonies, or an arangetram, among many other examples, people dance in such a way as to become someone or something else, to try on or feel out a different way of being. These experiments could produce sustained change, or they could dwell in memory as momentary expansions or reversals of identity.

Sometimes such experiments are formalized on the concert stage, where movement is performed that has been choreographed to construct a particular vision of the world and the relations of its inhabitants. These speculative forms of dancing introduce new inventions in ways of moving and interacting and sometimes new images of what the world could afford. Viewers can also project themselves into those roles, imagining what they might experience in those worlds.

As developed through screen technologies and social media, dancing also affords opportunities to augment one's social status through trendsetting, style influencing, and the possibility of becoming a celebrity. In short format platforms such as Instagram and TikTok, dancing can reach thousands or even millions of viewers. Some of these dances challenge viewers to create their own versions, forming a kind of movement discussion among otherwise strangers. The screen itself strongly privileges the visual appearance of the dancing, and it demands clear, striking shapes that can be sequenced to impress or surprise viewers, illustrate the lyrics in the music, introduce new possible ways of moving, or all of these. As L. Archer Porter (Nebraska-based settler-scholar) argues, various genres of screen dance afford an experience of intimacy, or what she calls an "intimaesthetics," in which the combined operations of camera operator, setting, dancer, and posting work to construct forms of authenticity entirely different from what the live experience of viewing dance affords.[39]

Other practices of dancing are specifically charged with memorating the past in an effort to affirm and preserve social values and beliefs. Dancing can be said to afford remembering insofar as the enacting of specific patterns of movement accesses events deemed to have occurred in the past, or dancing's patterns of movement enable dancers to summon up and commune with ancestors and past events. Often the knowledge about the past that dancing affords is experienced as sacred or otherwise irrefutable, in part because of the full body's active participation. Such knowledge is also experienced as especially foundational and profound because it takes place through the act of moving rather than through speaking or reading. The body's intense participation confirms the experience of the essentialness of this way of knowing.

Still other practices of dancing serve to sequester knowledge and provide solidarity in the face of colonial and other forms of domination. As referenced earlier, many Native dances are not only hidden from non-Native viewers but also require lengthy induction into their meanings. Thinking quite differently about what dancing does, three of the Native dancers from Cody's Wild West show utilized the newly minted technology of film, allowing Thomas Edison to document them dancing a prairie chicken dance. As Tria Blu Wakpa (Filipina, white, and unenrolled tribal member) explains, the dancers, calculating the camera's view, organized their floor path and incorporated North American Hand Talk, a way of communicating silently through gestures, to both threaten viewers with the prospect of revenge and satirize their conceptions of Native "savagery."[40] She argues that the dancers, having comprehended the durability of the new medium of film, also decided to send a message to future generations about the vitality of Native identity.

A different kind of rebelliousness was exercised by plantation slaves throughout the rural south, who devised choreography that exaggerated pompous and frivolous characteristics of white social dance etiquette, thereby giving them a conspiratorial togetherness and a momentary sense of agentic command over their own movements.[41] Where the parodical slave dances were hidden from the owners, in apartheid South Africa from the 1950s to '80s, Black mine workers were coerced into performing in a local stadium on Sundays, their one day off, for the entertainment and amusement of white onlookers, both locals and tourists.[42] While mine owners reasoned that the dancing would display the general contentment and well-being of the miners while at the same time exhausting them so as to ensure against any form of rebellion, the dancing may have offered the workers a source of pleasure and camaraderie through the exchange of dances from their various communities and through the humorous exaggeration of their seemingly wild appearance.

Dancing can also afford opportunities for more pointed forms of protest against existing social policies and other forms of discrimination. Martin proposes that dancing galvanizes the body in a way that potentially builds political will and momentum for what he calls "mobilization."[43] Dancing boosts the feeling of putting the body on the line. Because of this, dancing appears at political rallies and protests, where it affords vital commitment and togetherness. Black Lives Matter rallies have witnessed numerous eruptions of dancing as a form of both jubilation and defiance.[44] Sometimes planned in advance and other times coming together spontaneously as part of a gathering or march, dancers have sourced the Electric Slide, voguing, and twerking, among other forms. At Black Lives Matter events in Minneapolis, the group Kalpulli Yaocenoxtli, performing Mexican Nahua dances, regularly joins in, while worldwide circulation of the protests on social media sweep into the mix, among others, Aotearoa Māori dancers performing haka.

During the monthslong protest against the oil pipeline at Standing Rock, dances took place as part of ceremonies adjacent to where the water protectors had gathered, serving to support their actions by inspiring onlookers and invigorating those who were protesting. They also inserted themselves into the protest itself at one point, during a heated confrontation between water protectors and police. Appearing on a bluff above the protest, a large number of jingle dancers processed down the hill and, as Tiffany Midge (Hunkpapa Lakota enrolled member of the Standing Rock Sioux) describes it, the "dancers gathered on the main highway and took to the front lines, dancing about 150 yards away from where roughly nine armored police vehicles remained behind a wall of concrete barriers."[45] Confronting Humvees, military vehicles, and over three hundred heavily armed officers, the dancers continued to dance, slowly calming the situation while healing the water protectors. In these and many other examples, what dancing affords is both solidarity and resistance to subordination and an affirmation of the right to assert one's own physicality.

Dancing vivifies the experience of bodiliness and the immediacy of movement itself. The what-if in the impulse to move is actualized moment after moment. What if the weight shifts this way; what if the spin happens with a tilted head; what if the arm reaches in this direction; what if the step lands just before the downbeat? The realization of such what-ifs produces a sense of empowerment, wholeness, communion, connection, delight, and playfulness. It equally can afford an awareness of incapacity, ineffectualness, alienation, isolation, and loss. These what-ifs can provide entrance into otherworldly alternatives to daily life both as individuals and as a group. They can also offer affirmation of the moment in which movement is occurring, and, as I have tried to show, create knowledge of immense complexity. Preeminently, dancing affords the experience of the mind-filled body as a set of relations, coordinating with one another.

Because the theory of affordances emphasizes the notion that what one perceives in the world are the ways one can act in it, it proposes a paradigm of what experience is that is not based in stillness and stasis but rather in the ongoingness of movement. If a theory of what knowledge is can be based in the flux of reality and knowing can be embraced as a process that is always in motion, then dancing, an activity that foregrounds affordances themselves, also affords a modeling for how inquiry can take place. Dancing synthesizes critical reflection with imagining and investigating. It demands continual awareness of what movement is taking place but also how that movement, with its concomitant knowledge of the world, is emerging. Dancing makes evident the fact that its emergence cannot be separated from the world in which it comes into being. It both produces and reflects on connectedness.

CONTINUING ON . . .

I had walked with Simpson and Watts companioning me for many months when one day, passing under a magnificent live oak tree, a small fallen branch attached itself to my walking stick and joined me for some distance. When it came loose, I turned back to look at the tree, realizing, hoping, that it wanted to become friends. Since that day I have stopped and communed with the tree every time I take that walk. It has shared with me much about the calming shelter it provides and a peace that comes from standing quietly underneath it.

Recently, I had the opportunity to revisit the walks on Chumash lands that I took daily for several years. I was overwhelmed by the memories of those walks flooding in as I passed a particular bend or climb on the trail. Unusually verdant after two years of abundant rainfall, the chaparral was cluttered with clumps of flowers and their scents. Bold patterns of lichens covered rocks that were previously too dry to host them. I stopped suddenly at the curve where years earlier I had seen the dead fox. Knowing what I do now, I would have sat with the fox that morning, kept it company, and wished it well on its onward journey.

On another of the regular walks I have taken over the course of writing and rewriting this book, a small community of hill walkers has formed—those of us who see each other often, if not daily, on the fire road. Many of these folks also walk with their dogs, and one is a dog walker who shouts to, cuddles, scratches, and fondles her charges. Another runs the hills with his dog's leash strapped to his waist. He waves at me with both hands. Another recently walked the whole road with me, conferring about the UC campuses to which her daughter had been accepted. Some of these walkers are very knowledgeable about flora and fauna. One mentioned to me recently that a red-tailed hawk has moved into the canyon alongside the Cooper's hawks.

We nod to one another as we pass or, often, stop to chat for a minute or two. One woman is originally from Bangalore; another is Italian by birth; another moved from Sweden. We comment on the weather or share our anxieties about the election, the war in Ukraine, or the situation in Israel-Palestine, or our devotion to living in California. We trade tips on movies or theater or TV shows.

I haven't seen for some time now the diligent caretaker of two vizslas who often asks me to help by trying to distract them, or the proud new father of Poppy, who perches facing forward in his chest carrier, or the man who walks while balancing a plastic bottle full of water on his head, or the very polite bicyclist with the British accent.

A few weeks ago a whole team of intrepid weed whackers was standing at the top of a very steep hill about to mow down all the grasses on its slope in anticipation of fire season. I got to thank them for their work. The next day I saw them on a different ridge, and we all waved to each other.

The other day I stopped to talk to a young woman I sometimes see. I asked her if she knew what makes the skinny curving trails in the dirt that start to appear this time of year. She replied that it might be snails, adding that she often walks so early in the morning that she sees them. I told her I thought that if anyone would know, it would be her. She grinned, and we wished each other a good day.

One older couple I regularly see — Rita, who wants to live to be 106, and Gilbert, who is currently 89 — I first met when they were wearing MAGA hats that, on closer inspection, read, "Make America Gay Again." They have now been to my house for dinner. And Gilbert, who is a photographer, took the photo that is featured on the cover of this book.

Tiny threads of connection continually sprouting more.

And now the horrendous wildfires of January 2025 have come and gone. Our beloved fire road closed for a few weeks, and we all had to find other places to walk. Finally the road reopened, massively pummeled by the bulldozers that had widened and flattened it. But we are all back walking again, happy to feel the dirt and see each other.

NOTES

Essaying

1. Here, I am referencing Charles Sepulveda's (Tongva and Acjachemen) theorizing of the Tongva notion of *kuuyam*, or a person practicing respect for the land and all its inhabitants. Sepulveda, "Our Sacred Waters."
2. I am focusing on the term *connectedness* to align with Vine Deloria's (Standing Rock Sioux) and Leanne Betasamosake Simpson's (Michi Saagiig Nishnaabeg) emphasis on connection, while also distinguishing it from the term *relationality*, used frequently and with a wide variety of applications throughout Native and Indigenous studies scholarship. See Deloria, *Spirit and Reason*, and Simpson, "Land as Pedagogy." For me the action of connecting implies more movement than that of relationing or the "intra-activity" used by scholars such as Karen Barad (California-based settler-scholar) in "Posthumanist Performativity." Related metaphors, such as "braiding," used by Dwayne Donald (Beaver Hills Cree) and Robin Wall Kimmerer (Potawatomi), are also similar and identify the action. See Donald, "Forts, Curriculum, and Indigenous Métissage," and Kimmerer, *Braiding Sweetgrass*. For a lucid summary of Native and Indigenous scholars using *relationality*, see Shea Murphy (California-based settler-scholar), *Dancing Indigenous Worlds*, 1–3.
3. For a highly instructive discussion of the terminology *Native* and *Indigenous*, see Shea Murphy, *Dancing Indigenous Worlds*, 32–38.
4. Championing the work of Maxine Sheets-Johnstone (unmarked) as more radical than enactivist cognitive science, Michele Merritt (unmarked) argues that dance is a form of thinking in "Thinking-Is-Moving." My approach differs from hers in that I am trying to examine potential resonances among multiple disciplines, and I am arguing that moving in any amount or form is thought filled.
5. Paul Anthony Chambers (Colombia-based settler-scholar), in his critique of decolonial scholars' use of Descartes, has usefully contextualized Descartes's writings, arguing that his work actually served to support the feminist and antiracist progressive thinking of his time. Chambers, "Epistemology and Domination." Because of this I prefer using Cartesian epistemology as a way to refer to a broad set of assumptions about

mind and body as separate and charged with the distinct functions of cognition and action.

6. Foundational texts in this inquiry include Said (Palestinian American), *Orientalism*; Santos (Portuguese), *Epistemologies of the South*; and Tuck (Unangax̂) and Yang (diaspora settler of color), "Decolonization Is Not a Metaphor," 1–40.

7. For example, Eve Tuck and K. Wayne Yang in "Decolonization Is Not a Metaphor" argue strongly that decolonization pertains exclusively to the repatriation of Native Lands. In contrast, as Max Liboiron (Red River Métis/Michif and settler) asserts, anticolonial arguments and practices address ways of confronting colonization and attempting to establish more equitable relations. See Liboiron, *Pollution Is Colonialism*, 129–34.

8. In identifying tribal, ethnic, and other regional and national affiliations, I am following Liboiron's argument for documenting those who self-identify with a given group and those (unmarked) who feel no need or desire to do so. See Liboiron, *Pollution Is Colonialism*, 3–4. I am also using *settler-scholar* to identify non-Native authors who acknowledge their status as settlers. I am not using any of these affiliations as a way to certify authenticity. Burkhart (Cherokee), for example, discusses the settler-colonial tendency to require an authentic voice from Native speakers in contrast to Western philosophers who are not required to manifest such assurances in order to be interpreted as speaking the truth. See Burkhart, *Indigenizing Philosophy*, xxi, 73–79. Rather, my aim, in line with Liboiron, is to continually mark the privilege assumed by those who feel no such need. My sincerest apologies to anyone for whom I have provided an incorrect affiliation.

9. Wilson (Opaskwayak Cree), *Research Is Ceremony*, 7.

10. Tynan (Pairrebenne Trawlwoolway), "What Is Relationality?," 599–601.

11. Simpson identifies the following aspects of developing connection: (1) observation; (2) patience in apprehending what one is observing and all its surrounding context; (3) creativity in devising a connection to what one is observing; a connection that is "based on mutual respect, reciprocity, and caring," a connection that sustains and promotes all life, rather than privileging some life or other life; (4) sharing this connection with trusted others; (5) building on that connection in ways that mutually benefit everyone; and (6) using "ceremony, ritual, and the embodiment of teachings one already carries" to strengthen new connections and the relations they make possible. Simpson, "Land as Pedagogy," 10.

12. Simpson, "Land as Pedagogy," 12.

13. See also Tinker (Osage), "Stones Shall Cry Out," 119.

14. This process can be seen as the very act of theorizing. See Absolon (Anishinaabekwe), *Kaandossiwin*, for one compelling discussion of this.

15. In positioning myself and especially in asserting my white privilege, I am very mindful of the ways that reflexive methodologies can serve either to reclaim and reassert privilege or, alternatively, to absolve the author of blame. See Gani (South Asian–British) and Khan (South Asian–British), "Positionality Statements."

16. For more on developing relations and being a good student within Native contexts, see Shea Murphy, *Dancing Indigenous Worlds*, 272–80.

17. Shea Murphy provides a comprehensive discussion of similarities between Native studies and dance studies as scholars in both fields work to navigate and contest the colonial assumptions within the Academy. She also identifies clear differences between the two disciplines that, because of their distinctive blind spots, could make them strong and productive allies. See Shea Murphy, *Dancing Indigenous Worlds*, 27–64.

18. Watts (Anishinaabe and Haudenosaunee), "Indigenous Place-Thought and Agency," 23.

19. Watts, "Indigenous Place-Thought and Agency," 23.

20. Watts, "Indigenous Place-Thought and Agency," 28.

21. Stacy Alaimo (Oregon-based settler-scholar), quoted in Watts, "Indigenous Place-Thought and Agency," 29.

22. Burkhart uses the term *word warriors* in *Indigenizing Philosophy*, 147–50.

23. See Liboiron, *Pollution Is Colonialism*, 22.

24. Noudelmann (unmarked), "Literature," 203–16.

25. Wiedorn (unmarked), "Édouard Glissant's Archipelagic Thought," 3.

26. Hauʻofa (Tongan and Fijian), "Our Sea of Islands," 148–61.

27. Scholars such as Christina Sharpe (Black American) and Tiffany Lethabo King (Black American) have also contributed highly significant theorizations of the sea and the events taking place on and in it. Focusing on the Middle Passage, Sharpe identifies the ship, the hold, the wake, and the weather as metaphors that elucidate the enduring operations of anti-Black racism that are so pervasive throughout US culture today. King considers shoals, the shifting formations of sand and rock lying just beneath the water's surface, as inhibiting the free passage of ships, slowing them down and compounding the dangers of the sea, making movement as usual impossible. Both scholars invoke these aspects of the sea and travel across it to reflect on the persistent racism animating contemporary society and to assess possibilities for livability within it. Sharpe, *In the Wake*, and King, *Black Shoals*.

28. In my references to Land, I am following Styres (Mohawk, English, and French), Haig-Brown (Euro-Canadian settler-scholar), and Blimkie (Canadian settler-scholar), who argue that *land* (the more general term) refers to landscapes as affixed geographical and physical spaces that include earth, rocks, and waterways, whereas *Land* (the proper name) extends beyond a material fixed space. Land is a spiritually infused place grounded in interconnected and interdependent relationships and cultural positioning, and is highly contextualized. Styres et al., "Toward a Pedagogy of Land," 300–301. Liboiron makes a similar distinction in *Pollution Is Colonialism*, 7.

29. For an insightful discussion of how situatedness could be claimed while still dwelling in an episteme of coloniality, see Burkhart *Indigenizing Philosophy*, 64–67.

30. Harjo (Mvskoke), *Spiral to the Stars*; Recollet (Cree), "Gesturing Indigenous Futurities"; and Blu Wakpa (Filipina, white, and unenrolled tribal member), "Buffalo Dance," among many others. See also Shea Murphy, *Dancing Indigenous Worlds*, 221–25, for a discussion of Indigenous notions of futurity in relation to Afrofuturism. Shea Murphy also makes the point that the kinds of precarity facing the world today are

not new to Native peoples, whose entire world was destroyed during colonization. See *Dancing Indigenous Worlds*, 217–21.

31. Roy (South Asian), "Pandemic Is a Portal."

Walking as Place-Making

1. This is Edward Casey's (unmarked) term for our relationship to place, used throughout *Getting Back into Place*.

2. A major figure in this literature and source of inspiration for this work is Timothy Ingold (Britain-based settler-scholar). His various essays on walking (see Ingold, "Culture on the Ground," and Ingold, "Footprints Through the Weather-World") and his anthology, *Ways of Walking*, edited with Jo Lee Vergunst (Scotland-based settler-scholar), have been pathbreaking and deeply insightful. Additional approaches with which this work moves in tandem include Wylie (Britain-based settler-scholar), "Single Day's Walking"; Middleton (Britain-based settler-scholar), "Sense and the City"; Wunderlich (Britain-based settler-scholar), "Walking and Rhythmicity"; and Seamon (United States–based settler-scholar), *Geography of the Lifeworld*.

3. Simpson, "Land as Pedagogy"; Harjo, *Spiral to the Stars*; Burkhart, *Indigenizing Philosophy*; Haraway (California-based settler-scholar), "Situated Knowledges"; and Harding (California-based settler-scholar), *Science Question in Feminism*.

4. Almost all the descriptions of my surroundings refer to walks taken on the Tongva Land now known as the Hollywood Hills in what the Spanish conquistadors named Los Angeles. A few of the descriptions reference Chumash territory in what is now called Ojai, California, and the Inconsolables is a mountain range in Paiute territory in the Eastern Sierra.

5. Kirkman (unmarked), *Pictorial and Historical Map*.

6. Sepulveda, "Our Sacred Waters," 46.

7. Doti (California-based settler-scholar), "Spanish California Missions." See also Hyslop (settler-scholar), *Contest for California*, and Lightfoot, *Indians, Missionaries, and Merchants*.

8. UCLA, Mapping Indigenous LA, "Visit Our Story Maps."

9. Mason (United States–based settler-scholar) argues that "Fages' Code of Conduct" from 1787, authored by the commanding officer of the region, Pedro Fages, reflects a restraint in approaching Native people based on his extensive battles with Apaches and Navajos. Fages advised settlers not to allow any Native peoples into their houses and to avoid their dances since they amassed large numbers of participants who could be turned against the soldiers. Mason, "Fages' Code of Conduct."

10. UCLA, Mapping Indigenous LA, "Visit Our Story Maps."

11. UCLA, Mapping Indigenous LA, "Visit Our Story Maps."

12. Weighill (Chumash), "2-Step Tales of Hahashka," 150–57.

13. Duane (California-based settler-scholar), "People's History."

14. Tuck and Yang, "Decolonization Is Not a Metaphor," 14–17.

15. Tuck et al., "Introduction," 16.

16. Barrett (unmarked), *Beyond the Brain*, 165.

17. Anderson (unmarked), *After Phrenology*, 181–82.

18. Anderson, *After Phrenology*, 177–78.

19. Piaget (unmarked) was an early exponent of this understanding of how cognition develops through bodily movement. For more on the neurological aspects of how these patterns develop, see Pfeifer (unmarked) and Bongard (unmarked), *How the Body Shapes*, 169.

20. Gibson (unmarked), *Senses Considered*, 285.

21. Rifkin (New York–based settler-scholar), *Beyond Settler Time*, 29.

22. Vergunst notes, following Lefebvre's (unmarked) notion of rhythm, that finding the rhythm of walking does not mean repeating each step exactly. Rather, rhythm is only established when there is variation, and this is certainly the case when walking. Vergunst, "Taking a Trip," 116.

23. I will expand on this idea, engaging much more directly with the disability literature, in the last essay in this volume.

24. The fact that these distinctions even exist is a product of the colonial epistemology through which the various academic disciplines have been established and distinguished from one another.

25. Young (Chicago-based settler-scholar), "Throwing like a Girl," 147.

26. Sekimoto (Asian American) and Brown (Black American), *Race and the Senses*, 3.

27. Goeman (Seneca), "From Place to Territories," 25.

28. To propose that there are social as well as physical affordances is not incompatible with Bourdieu's (unmarked) habitus. Both assume that the social consists of orchestrated patterns of behavior that are learned from birth. And both emphasize the improvised nature of the daily remaking of habits, protocols, strictures, and possible courses of action. However, the ways that Bourdieu's habitus has been applied often assume that it is a system that is imposed. Similarly, Foucault's (unmarked) theory of discipline is often regarded as an exercise in power that comes from above. What the concept of social affordances enables is a reevaluation of this notion of culture as inflicted and enforced by some outside forces. It also establishes a connection between the perceptual field and its social meanings. See Bourdieu, "Structures and the Habitus," and Foucault, *Discipline and Punish*.

29. Tuck-Po (Malaysian), "Before a Step Too Far."

30. Gooch (Sweden-based settler-scholar), "Feet Following Hooves."

31. For a cogent analysis of the history of Benjamin's (unmarked) writing on the flaneur, see McDonough (unmarked), "Crimes of the Flaneur." Hammergren (Sweden-based settler-scholar) appropriates the term, changing its gender and adding kinesthesia to the sense modalities of the walker, in her essay "The Re-Turn of the Flâneuse."

32. Solnit (United States–based settler-scholar), *Wanderlust*.

33. Cervenak (North Carolina–based settler-scholar), *Wandering*.

34. On the need to police the movements of Black slaves, see also King, *Black Shoals*, 106–10.

35. See Christopher Brown's vivid firsthand account of a police interrogation for a much more detailed description of the affordances and responses he experienced in that encounter, in Sekimoto and Brown, *Race and the Senses*, 63–85.

36. Fanon (French Afro-Caribbean), *Black Skin, White Masks*.

37. Certeau (unmarked), *Practice of Everyday Life*.

38. Lefebvre, *Production of Space*, 93.

39. Sepulveda, "Our Sacred Waters."

40. See also Castañeda (Tejano), "Engendering the History."

41. Ingold, "Culture on the Ground," 321.

42. Carter (Australia-based settler-scholar), *Road to Botany Bay*. Laying the groundwork for Carter's argument, Casey has traced the increasing predominance of space over place in Western philosophical thought, showing how, by the seventeenth century, space as an abstract and empty void came to triumph over experiences of place. See Casey, *Fate of Place*.

43. In reflecting on his thirty years of walking in and around Palestine, Raja Shehadeh (Palestinian) reminisces about the centuries old homesteads nestled in to folds in the hills, each with its terraced gardens and carefully planted olive trees, now bulldozed through by roads that carve up the Land, erase footpaths, and compromise wadis. These roads transport the materials for constructing new settlements, mostly built on the crests of hills to survey the landscape and effectively defend claims of ownership against those who would necessarily approach from below. Similarly, the Lands of Indigenous peoples worldwide have been sliced through, enclosed, and partitioned by roads that establish new borders and boundaries. See Shehadeh, *Palestinian Walks*.

44. Ingold and Vergunst, *Ways of Walking*, 13–14.

45. Cajete (Tewa), *Native Science*, 186.

46. Cajete, *Native Science*, 188.

47. Welch (California-based settler-scholar), "Brief History," 6.

48. Max Liboiron discusses how the researchers in his laboratory are discouraged from wearing earbuds to listen to music or other programs because it fails to pay full and due respect to the dead animals they are dissecting. He considers this part of a protocol that helps to establish respectful relations among all beings. Liboiron, *Pollution Is Colonialism*, 122–24.

49. See Sepulveda, "Our Sacred Waters," 52–56.

50. Pfeifer and Bongard, *How the Body Shapes*, 295–98.

51. Dijkstra, Kaschak, and Zwaan (all unmarked) in "Body Posture," for example, show how a person's postural positioning of the body enhances the retrieval of memories from that person's past.

52. Fabian (unmarked), *Time and the Other*, 4–18.

53. Cajete, *Native Science*, 184.

54. Allice Legat (Canada-based settler-scholar), among others, explains this practice in her book, *Walking the Land, Feeding the Fire*.

55. Goeman, "From Place to Territories."

56. Ingold and Vergunst, *Ways of Walking*, 5–6.
57. Basso (Connecticut-based settler-scholar), "'Speaking with Names,'" 106.
58. Garroutte (Cherokee) and Westcott (Anishinaabe and Cree), "Story Is a Living Being," 68.
59. Van Dooren (Australia-based settler-scholar) and Rose (Australia-based settler-scholar), "Storied-Places."
60. See Vergunst for a marvelously detailed analysis of the differences between slipping and tripping, and how they illuminate what walking entails. Vergunst, "Taking a Trip," 109–11.
61. Casey, *Fate of Place*, 202–42.
62. Gros (unmarked), *Philosophy of Walking*.
63. Husserl (unmarked), "World of the Living Present."
64. Casey, *Fate of Place*, 219.
65. Merleau-Ponty (unmarked) as cited in Casey, *Fate of Place*, 232.
66. Casey, *Getting Back into Place*, 63.
67. Casey, *Getting Back into Place*, 70–82.
68. Casey, *Getting Back into Place*, 94.
69. Ahmed (Pakistani British), *Queer Phenomenology*.
70. Benveniste (unmarked), *Problems in General Linguistics*, 223–30.

Being, Knowing, and Acting

1. Merleau-Ponty, *Visible and the Invisible*, 139–40.
2. Burkhart's notion of locality embraces all three areas. He writes, "Locality . . . is the originary and continuing manifestation of being, knowing, and morality through the land." Burkhart, *Indigenizing Philosophy*, 227.
3. Burkhart points to the strong tendency among Western scholars to imagine that Native thinking is transparent and easily graspable. Burkhart, *Indigenizing Philosophy*, 180–81.
4. Tinker further argues that if we cannot determine what consciousness is, how can we accord humans consciousness while simultaneously denying consciousness to other entities? Tinker, "Stones Shall Cry Out."
5. Burkhart, "'Locality Is a Metaphysical Fact.'" See also Burkhart, *Indigenizing Philosophy*.
6. Harjo, *Spiral to the Stars*, 155.
7. Hokowhitu (Māori, Ngāti Pūkenga) argues that knowledge and selfhood are produced through interaction with the immediacy of everyday experience. Hokowhitu, "Indigenous Existentialism and the Body."
8. Native scholars have pointed to the similarities between new materialist and Native conceptions of the material world, arguing that "ignoring the thousand year old knowledge tradition . . . in favor of only citing and focusing on new materialist thinkers would have the effect of erasing, yet again, Native values." Rosiek et al. (United States–based settler-scholars), "New Materialisms," 333.

9. Barad (California-based settler-scholar), "Posthumanist Performativity," 815.
10. Barad, "Posthumanist Performativity," 815–19.
11. Barad, "Posthumanist Performativity," 824.
12. Shildrick (unmarked), *Embodying the Monster*, 114–18.
13. Merleau-Ponty designates "not matter nor mind, nor substance, but an elemental medium—like air or fire—in which self and world are constituted in mutual relation. Merleau-Ponty, *Visible and the Invisible*, 139–40.
14. Casey, *Fate of Place*, 219.
15. Merleau-Ponty, quoted in Casey, *Fate of Place*, 232.
16. Gibson, *Ecological Approach*, 128.
17. Chemero (unmarked), *Radical Embodied Cognitive Science*, 196.
18. Gibson, *Ecological Approach*, 135.
19. Young, "Throwing like a Girl," 145–48.
20. Watts, "Indigenous Place-Thought and Agency," 21.
21. See Burkhart's discussion of Native ways of knowing in *Indigenizing Philosophy*, 120–60.
22. Burkhart, *Indigenizing Philosophy*, 195.
23. Simpson, "Land as Pedagogy," 12.
24. Simpson, "Land as Pedagogy," 7.
25. This process can be seen as the very act of theorizing or as what Kathleen E. Absolon refers to as "re-search."
26. Burkhart, *Indigenizing Philosophy*, 196.
27. Burkhart, *Indigenizing Philosophy*, 196.
28. Burkhart, *Indigenizing Philosophy*, 35.
29. Gibson, *Ecological Approach*, 258.
30. Seeking to refine further how the organism and the environment together construct meaning, Baggs (unmarked) and Chemero propose a distinction between the species niche and an organism's *Umwelt*, or individually specific history of experience. Entering the cockpit of a plane, for example, is meaningful to a trained pilot in a way that it is not for a child. Baggs and Chemero, "Third Sense of Environment," 9.
31. Barad, "Posthumanist Performativity," 829.
32. Leroy Little Bear (Blackfoot) makes the point that all of matter is both mingled and in motion in "Traditional Knowledge and Humanities," 521.
33. Deloria, *Spirit and Reason*, 34.
34. Kimmerer, *Braiding Sweetgrass*, 346–47.
35. The full quote in Deloria, *Spirit and Reason*, 47, reads:

> There is a proper way to live in the universe: There is a content to every action, behavior, and belief. . . . There is a direction to the universe, empirically exemplified in the physical growth cycles of childhood, youth, and old age, with the corresponding responsibility of every entity to enjoy life, fulfill itself, and increase in wisdom and the spiritual development of personality. Nothing has incidental meaning and there are no coincidences. . . .

In the moral universe all activities, events, and entities are related, and consequently it does not matter what kind of existence an entity enjoys, for the responsibility is always there for it to participate in the continuing creation of reality.

36. For a much fuller and deeply insightful discussion of the relationship between knowing and ethical action, see Burkhart, *Indigenizing Philosophy*, 271–306.

37. Aileen Moreton-Robinson (Goenpul, Quandamooka First Nation) expands on this proposal, explaining that "relationality is grounded in a holistic conception of the inter-connectedness and inter-substantiation between and among all living things and the earth, which is inhabited by a world of ancestors and creator beings. It informs our epistemological and ethical premise that social research should begin with an awareness of our proper relationships with the world we inhabit, and is conducted with respect, responsibility, generosity, obligation, and reciprocity." Moreton-Robinson, "Relationality," 70. Here Moreton-Robinson stresses the ethical dimension of social research and the necessity to enter into respectful reciprocal relations with any object of study.

38. Burkhart, "'Locality Is a Metaphysical Fact,'" 6.

39. Wynter (Jamaican) elaborates extensively on Dussel's claim that conquest preceded Cartesian claims to rationality through a close analysis of the various stages through which the Spanish nation-state needed to rationalize the seizure of lands in the New World and enslave or enserf its inhabitants. Specifically, she focuses on the debates between Bartolomé de las Casas (unmarked) and Juan Ginés de Sepúlveda (unmarked) that eventually resolved in the establishment of the Chain of Being, a framework that leaned heavily on the assertion of the superiority of rationality as embodied within Europeans, and the concomitant assertions that Africans were barely superior to animals and Native peoples were hierarchically slightly superior, hence educatable and convertible to Christianity. See Wynter, "Unsettling the Coloniality of Being."

40. Ingold, "Culture on the Ground," 321.

41. Burkhart, *Indigenizing Philosophy*, 33–44.

42. Burkhart's discussion of the ego constituo includes a fascinating argument about Locke, whose work as secretary to Lord Shaftesbury and the Lords Proprietors of Carolina consisted of providing a justification for appropriation of colonial land without Native consent. Burkhart, *Indigenizing Philosophy*, 33–44.

43. Gibson, *Ecological Approach*, 31.

44. Simpson, "Land as Pedagogy," 12.

45. In their research on the amount of plastic in cod, Liboiron has instituted a number of ethical practices in the lab that include asking for permission to remove fish from the ocean and not wearing headphones when dissecting a fish in order not to be walled off from it. Researchers also return the remains of the fish to the ocean so that they can provide sustenance for other life forms living with the cod. See Liboiron, *Pollution Is Colonialism*, 122–24.

Embodying the Decolonial

Epigraphs: The full quote in Di Paolo and Thompson, "The Enactive Approach," 68, reads as follows:

> Embodied approaches to cognition hold that the body is crucial for cognition. Yet despite many decades of research, what this "embodiment thesis" (Wilson and Foglia, 2011) amounts to still remains unclear, as the present volume with its diverse range of contributions indicates (see also Shapiro, 2011). How to interpret the embodiment thesis depends on how to interpret the meanings of its key terms, "body" and "cognition," as well as on what it means exactly to say that the body is "crucial" for cognition... [Kyselo and Di Paolo, "Locked-in Syndrome." In recent years, the term "embodied" has been used elastically to refer to anything from conservative ideas about how bodily action provides a format for neuronal representations (Goldman and de Vignemont, 2009; Gallese, 2010; Goldman, 2012) or helps to reduce computational load (Clark, 2008; Wheeler, 2005, 2010; Wilson, 2004), to a variety of "radical embodiment" (Clark, 1999; Thompson and Varela, 2001) proposals—for example, that kinesthetic body schemas are a constitutive part of mental skills (Lakoff and Johnson, *Philosophy in the Flesh*; Núñez, 2010), that sensorimotor know-how is a constitutive part of perceptual experience (O'Regan and Noë, 2001; Noë, 2004), that bodily life regulation is a constitutive part of phenomenal consciousness and its extended neurophysiological substrates (Thompson and Varela, 2001; Thompson and Cosmelli, 2011), and that social sensorimotor interaction can be a constitutive part of social cognition (De Jaegher, Di Paolo, and Gallagher, 2010).

The full quote in Sheets-Johnstone, "Emotion and Movement, 275, reads as follows:

> The penchant to talk about and to explain ourselves and/or aspects of ourselves as embodied—as in "embodied connectionism" (Bechtel, 1997), and even as in "embodied mind" (Varela et al., 1991; Lakoff and Johnson, 1999), "embodied schema"(Johnson, 1987), "embodied agents," "embodied actions" (Varela, 1999), and "phenomenological embodiment" (Lakoff and Johnson, 1999)—evokes not simply the possibility of a disembodied relationship and of near or outright tautologies as in "embodied agents," "embodied actions" and "the embodied mind is part of the living body" (Lakoff and Johnson, 1999, p. 565), but the spectre of Cartesianism. In this sense, the term "embodied" is a lexical band-aid covering a 350-year-old wound generated and kept suppurating by a schizoid metaphysics. It evades the arduous and (by human lifetime standards) infinite task of clarifying and elucidating the nature of living nature from the ground up.

1. Merleau-Ponty, *Phenomenology of Perception*; Beauvoir, "Littérature et métaphysique," "Que peut la littérature?" and "Mon expérience d'écrivain"; Young, "Throwing like a Girl"; Ahmed, *Queer Phenomenology*; and Csordas (California-based settler-scholar), *Body as Representation*.

2. Federici (New York–based settler-scholar), *Caliban and the Witch*; Hill (African American), *Black Feminist Thought*; and Anzaldúa (Xicana) and Moraga (Xicana), *This Bridge Called My Back*.

3. Sedgwick (unmarked), *Epistemology of the Closet*, and Garland-Thomson (Georgia-based settler-scholar), *Extraordinary Bodies*.

4. Migdalek (unmarked), *Embodied Performance of Gender*; Hawkesworth (unmarked), *Embodied Power*; Carolan (Colorado-based settler-scholar), *Embodied Food Politics*; Thanem (unmarked) and Knights (unmarked), *Embodied Research Methods*; and Tapias (Hispanic), *Embodied Protests*.

5. Anderson, *After Phrenology*; Barrett, *Beyond the Brain*; Chemero, *Radical Embodied Cognitive Science*; Pfeifer and Bongard, *How the Body Shapes*; and Thompson (unmarked), *Mind in Life*.

6. Haraway (California-based settler-scholar), "Situated Knowledges," and Harding (California-based settler-scholar), *Science Question in Feminism*.

7. Haraway, "Situated Knowledges," 581–82.

8. Grosz (North Carolina–based settler-scholar), *Volatile Bodies*; Halberstam (New York–based settler-scholar), *Female Masculinity*; and Butler (California-based settler-scholar), *Gender Trouble*.

9. "Practice," *Merriam Webster Dictionary*, https://www.merriam-webster.com/dictionary/practice.

10. Taylor (New York–based settler-scholar), *Archive and the Repertoire*.

11. Baggs et al., "Extended Skill Learning," 2.

12. Bourdieu, *Theory of Practice*, 89–92.

13. Bourdieu, *Theory of Practice*, 72–89.

14. Daniel (Black), *Dancing Wisdom*.

15. Rosa (Brazilian), *Brazilian Bodies*, 223.

16. Sweet (United States–based settler-scholar), *Dances of the Tewa Pueblo Indians*, 3, 10.

17. Sweet, *Dances of the Tewa Pueblo Indians*, 8, 24.

18. Sweet, *Dances of the Tewa Pueblo Indians*, 31, 34.

19. Sweet, *Dances of the Tewa Pueblo Indians*, 33–34.

20. Sweet, *Dances of the Tewa Pueblo Indians*, 29–30.

21. Weighill, "2-Step Tales of Hahashka," 49.

22. Weighill, "2-Step Tales of Hahashka," 51.

23. Weighill, "2-Step Tales of Hahashka," 47.

24. Weighill, "2-Step Tales of Hahashka," 71.

25. Shea Murphy, *People Have Never Stopped Dancing*.

26. Shea Murphy, *Dancing Indigenous Worlds*.

27. Garcia (Tewa), quoted in Sweet, *Dances of the Tewa Pueblo Indians*, 91.

28. Anderson, *After Phrenology*, 234–35.

29. Wacquant (California-based settler-scholar), "Flesh and Blood," 2.

30. Wacquant, "Flesh and Blood," 3.

31. Bennett (Maryland-based settler-scholar), *Vibrant Matter*, 23.

32. Wacquant (California-based settler-scholar), "Flesh and Blood"; Ingold, "Walking the Plank"; and Ness (California-based settler-scholar), "Dancing in the Field."

33. Anderson, *After Phrenology*, 177–78.

34. Landy (unmarked) and Goldstone (unmarked), "Proximity and Precedence in Arithmetic."

35. Anderson, *After Phrenology*, 184–85.

36. Anderson, *After Phrenology*, 181–82.

37. Grosfoguel (Puerto Rican), "Structure of Knowledge," 86.

38. Grosfoguel, "Structure of Knowledge," 76.

39. Wynter explains "that Man was to be invented in its first form as the rational political subject of the state, as one who displayed his reason by primarily adhering to the laws of the state—rather than, as before, in seeking to redeem himself from enslavement to Original Sin by primarily adhering to the prohibitions of the Church." Wynter, "Unsettling the Coloniality of Being," 277.

40. Wynter writes: "It was to be the peoples of the militarily expropriated New World territories (i.e., Indians), as well as the enslaved peoples of Black Africa (i.e., Negroes), that were made to reoccupy the matrix slot of Otherness—to be made into the physical referent of the idea of the irrational/subrational Human Other, to this first degodded (if still hybridly religio-secular) 'descriptive statement' of the human in history, as the descriptive statement that would be foundational to modernity." Wynter, "Unsettling the Coloniality of Being," 266.

41. Wynter, "1492."

42. See Wynter, "Unsettling the Coloniality of Being."

43. Grosfoguel, "Structure of Knowledge."

44. Examining in detail Southern Connecticut mapmaking procedures in colonial America, Pearce argues that colonists often incorporated Native names of landmarks and then added boundaries to enclose them. Pearce (Potawatomi), "Encroachment by Word."

45. Analyzing the arrival of the British in Australia, Paul Carter shows how mapmaking, a practice oblivious to the topographical nuances of a given terrain, transformed the waterways, hillocks, ravines, and plant life of Botany Bay into identical, measured parcels. See Carter, *Road to Botany Bay*.

46. Wynter expands on the concept of the *pieza* as introduced by C. L. R. James. See Wynter, "Master Conception."

47. For an insightful discussion of Native conceptions of the four directions and Native ways of orienting in the world, see Burkhart, *Indigenizing Philosophy*, 129–39.

Remembering Dancing

Parts of this essay also appear under the same title in Susanne Franco and Marina Nordera, eds., *The Oxford Handbook on Dance and Memory* (Oxford: Oxford University Press), forthcoming.

1. Connerton (unmarked), *How Modernity Forgets*.
2. Pfeifer and Bongard, *How the Body Shapes*, 303.
3. Basso, "Speaking with Names," 112.
4. Basso, "Speaking with Names," 108.
5. Weighill, "2-Step Tales of Hahashka," 56.
6. For a history of the development of ecological or enactivist approaches to cognitive science, see Thompson, *Mind in Life*. For various perspectives on the approach, see also Peeters (unmarked) and Segundo-Ortin (unmarked), "Misplacing Memories?"; Pfeifer and Bongard, *How the Body Shapes*; Chemero, *Radical Embodied Cognitive Science*; and Anderson, *After Phrenology*. In their recent work, "Extended Skill Learning," Baggs, Raja, and Anderson provide an excellent summary of the differences between the two theses and suggest a possible approach to their synthesis.
7. Sheets-Johnstone observes that the use of *motor* to describe muscle action is misleading and inaccurate. She proposes that the term should be *kinetic*, so *sensory-kinetic action* would be a better choice. However, since the literature refers repeatedly to *motor*, I will use it. Sheets-Johnstone, "Kinesthetic Memory," 76–77.
8. Barrett, *Beyond the Brain*, 186.
9. Anderson, *After Phrenology*, 230. Di Paolo and Thompson continue: "Given that sense-making is an embodied process of active regulation of the coupling between agent and world, social interaction—through patterns of bodily coordination and breakdown—opens the possibility of this process being shared among the interactors. This shared form of sense-making is what is meant by 'participatory sense-making.' It happens to various degrees, from orientation of individual sense-making (someone draws our attention to an aspect of the world we have ignored) to joint sense-making (a piece of work is literally created together through a process that would not be possible by the individuals involved on their own)." Di Paolo and Thompson, "Enactive Approach."
10. Quoted in Connerton, *How Modernity Forgets*, 92.
11. Fend et al. (unmarked), "Optimal Morphology."
12. For a complete description and discussion of the experiment, see Pfeifer and Bongard, *How the Body Shapes*, 295–98.
13. Dijkstra et al., "Body Posture."
14. For a comprehensive overview of these experiments, see Wilson (unmarked), "Sensorimotor Coding in Working Memory."
15. Yates (unmarked), *Art of Memory*.
16. Krokos et al. (unmarked), "Virtual Memory Palaces."
17. For a good overview of the research, see Heyes and Catmur (both unmarked), "What Happened to Mirror Neurons?" See also my discussion of the research on them in Foster (California-based settler-scholar), *Choreographing Empathy*, 121–25, 165–168.
18. Glenberg (unmarked), "What Memory Is For."
19. Rosenfield (unmarked), *Invention of Memory*, 163, and Edelman (unmarked), *Neural Darwinism*.
20. Edelman, *Neural Darwinism*, 241. Quoted in Pfeifer and Bongard, *How the Body Shapes*, 312.

21. De Brigard, "Is Memory for Remembering?," 25.

22. Pfeifer and Bongard, *How the Body Shapes*, 306–7.

23. See Baggs et al., "Extended Skill Learning," for an in-depth analysis of what a skill is.

24. Mauss (unmarked), "Techniques of the Body."

25. Giard (unmarked), "Nourishing Arts."

26. See Taylor, *Archive and the Repertoire*.

27. Dangeli (Tsimshian), "Dancing Chiax, Dancing Sovereignty," 78.

28. On the reconstruction of baroque opera ballets, see Turocy (unmarked), "Taught by Pygmalion," and Franko (unmarked), *Dancing Body in Renaissance Choreography*. A reconstruction of Nijinsky's *Rite of Spring* was undertaken by Kenneth Archer (unmarked) and Millicent Hodson (unmarked) and is documented in their book, *Lost Rite*.

29. Askren, "Dancing Our Stone Mask," 37.

30. For example, Choctaw author LeAnne Howe explains, "If worse comes to worst and our people forget where we left our stories, the birds will remember and bring them back to us." Quoted in Arnold (Sinixt Band of the Colville Confederated Tribes) and Pescaia (Hawaiian), "Considering the Revolution," 13. See also Mitchell (California-based settler-scholar) and Burelle (California-based settler-scholar), "*Dee(a)r Spine*."

31. Simpson, *As We Have Always Done*, 14–16.

32. Comanche tribal historian Jimmy Arterberry, as quoted in McBeth, "Memory, History, and Contested Pasts," 19.

33. Simpson, *As We Have Always Done*, 12.

34. For numerous literary examples of this, see Bernardin (Oregon-based settler-scholar), "Intergenerational Memory."

35. Miranda (Esselen and Chumash), "Saying the Padre Had Grabbed Her," 94.

36. Dewey's (unmarked) essay is commented on in Pfeifer and Bongard, *How the Body Shapes*, 120.

Dancing's Affordances

1. This is Véronique Doisneau's (unmarked) description of her role in *Swan Lake* as she describes it in Jérôme Bel's (unmarked) piece *Véronique Doisneau*.

2. See Johnson (Black), *Dark Matter*, ix–37, and DeFrantz (Black), "Breaking in My House."

3. Gibson, *Ecological Approach*, 114.

4. As Gibson notes, "Knowledge of the environment, surely, develops as perception develops, extends as the observers travel, gets finer as they learn to scrutinize, gets longer as they apprehend more events, gets fuller as they see more objects, and gets richer as they notice more affordances." Gibson, *Ecological Approach*, 126.

5. Sobchack (California-based settler-scholar), "Choreography for One," 59.

6. As Ward (unmarked) explains: "Avila lost his right leg and hip . . . to . . . a rare form of cancer" and now has what he "calls his 'new morphology,' a new way of look-

ing at his bodily material and technique. Small adjustments to balance executed in tiny shifts and jumps of his left foot, along with the precise counterbalance of his exquisitely refined arms, turn Avila's 'new morphology' into an incessant source of strength and beauty." See Ward, "Course in Miracles," 8.

7. Lee (California-based settler-scholar), "On with the Dance," 11.

8. Gibson explains that niches include "political and economic interactions as well as their sexual, nurturing, fighting, and cooperative behaviors." Gibson, *Ecological Approach*, 135.

9. Dokumaci (Canada-based settler-scholar), "People as Affordances," S104–S105.

10. Dokumaci, "People as Affordances," S106–S107.

11. Bell (United States–based settler-scholar) and Clegg (Texas-based settler-scholar, "Ecological Approach."

12. Kim (Asian American), "Crip-of-Color Critique," 2.

13. Kim, "Crip-of-Color Critique," 2.

14. Lovern (Georgia-based settler-scholar), "Native American Worldview," 114.

15. Lovern, "Indigenous Perspectives on Difference," 313.

16. Deloria likewise argues that kinship is charged with the responsibility to assist the "weak and helpless." Deloria, *Spirit and Reason*, 28.

17. Sobchack, "Choreography for One," 56.

18. Sheppard (Black Briton) used the pseudonym in a series of blog posts between 2006 and 2013. Quoted in Watts Belser (Washington, DC–based settler-scholar), "Vital Wheels," 10–11.

19. Johnson offers a detailed discussion of the ways that Black, Africanist, and diasporic values overlap and also compete with one another as claims for the origin of breaking. She argues that Africanist aesthetics are diasporic, having blended with many other diverse movement practices worldwide. See Johnson, *Dark Matter*, 52–57.

20. For in-depth studies of how dance produces certain social values, see Novack (New York–based settler-scholar), *Sharing the Dance*; Martin (New York–based settler-scholar), *Critical Moves*; and DeFrantz, *Dancing Revelations*, among others.

21. Wheelchair Dancer, quoted in Watts Belser, "Vital Wheels," 12.

22. Bennett, *Vibrant Matter*.

23. Watts Belser, "Vital Wheels," 13.

24. Watts Belser, "Vital Wheels," 12.

25. Gibson, *Ecological Approach*, 258.

26. Watts Belser, "Vital Wheels," 17–18.

27. Watts Belser, "Vital Wheels," 15–17.

28. For a discussion of some of these differences, see Foster, *Choreographing Empathy*, 18–23.

29. Jean-Noël Laurenti (unmarked) has pointed out the ways that dance notation facilitated the building of the French nation-state by assimilating all regional differences in dances into one overarching set of positions and steps. Laurenti, "Feuillet's Thinking." I have made a similar argument and also discussed how Feuillet notation inculcated an awareness of one's own location within a geometrized space in which

the "front" and "back" of a room came into existence and became more important than one's relative distance to all the others present. Foster, *Choreographing Empathy*, 23–26.

30. This is part of the argument for conserving disability made by Garland-Thomson (Georgia-based settler-scholar) in "Case for Conserving Disability."

31. Chemero, *Radical Embodied Cognitive Science*, 204.

32. See Johnson, *Dark Matter*, 40–52.

33. Both Peggy Phelan (California-based settler-scholar) in *Unmarked* and André Lepecki (New York–based settler-scholar) in *Of the Presence of the Body* champion dance's ephemerality, where Graham McFee (unmarked) in *Understanding Dance* is concerned that it weakens dance and that this incapacity could be strengthened through better practices of dance notation.

34. Sobchack, "Choreography for One," 58.

35. Anderson, *After Phrenology*, 245–80.

36. *Kinestheme* is Randy Martin's term for a generalized way of moving that identifies political and economic as well as aesthetic values built into it. See his "The Precarious Dance."

37. See McMaster's (Canadian and Plains Cree) website: http://merylmcmaster.com/.

38. See Heyes (unmarked) and Catmur (unmarked), "What Happened to Mirror Neurons?" See also Foster, *Choreographing Empathy*, 121–25, 165–68.

39. Porter (Nebraska-based settler-scholar), "Domestic Stage."

40. Blu Wakpa, "*Buffalo Dance*."

41. Stuckey (African American), *Slave Culture*.

42. Charlson (California-based settler-scholar), "Framing Black Labor," 9.

43. In *Valuing Dance* I argued that Martin's theory of mobilization might be one of dance's resourcefulnesses, the hypothetical capacity of dance to be tapped for the purposes of either gift giving or commodity production. Here I am focusing not on dance's potential but instead on what dancing can actually enact.

44. Burke (unmarked), "Dancing Bodies."

45. Midge, Tiffany (Hunkpapa Lakota enrolled member of the Standing Rock Sioux), "Thousands of Jingle Dress Dancers."

BIBLIOGRAPHY

Absolon, Kathleen E. *Kaandossiwin: How We Come to Know; Indigenous Re-Search Methodologies*. 2nd ed. Black Point, NS: Fernwood Publishing, 2022.

Ahmed, Sara. *Queer Phenomenology: Orientations, Objects, Others*. Durham, NC: Duke University Press, 2006.

Anderson, Michael L. *After Phrenology: Neural Reuse and the Interactive Brain*. Cambridge, MA: MIT Press, 2014.

Anzaldúa, Gloria, and Cherríe Moraga, eds. *This Bridge Called My Back: Writings by Radical Women of Color*. Watertown, MA: Persephone Press, 1981.

Arnold, Laurie, and Mikiʻala Ayau Pescaia. "Considering the Revolution: Indigenous Histories and Memory in Alaska, Hawaiʻi, and the Indigenous Plateau." *Public Historian* 43, no. 4 (November 1, 2021): 7–20. https://doi.org/10.1525/tph.2021.43.4.7.

Askren, Miqueʼl. "Dancing Our Stone Mask out of Confinement: A Twenty-First-Century Tsimshian Epistemology." In *Objects of Exchange: Social and Material Transformation on the Late Nineteenth-Century Northwest Coast*, edited by Aaron Glass. New York: Bard Graduate Center: Decorative Arts, Design History, Material Culture, 2011. Distributed by Yale University Press.

Baggs, Edward, and Anthony Chemero. "The Third Sense of Environment." In *Perception as Information Detection*, edited by Jeffrey B. Wagman and Julia J. C. Blau. Milton Park, UK: Routledge, 2019.

Baggs, Edward, Vicente Raja, and Michael L. Anderson. "Extended Skill Learning." *Frontiers in Psychology* 11 (August 14, 2020): 1956. https://doi.org/10.3389/fpsyg.2020.01956.

Barad, Karen. "Posthumanist Performativity: Toward an Understanding of How Matter Comes to Matter." *Signs: Journal of Women in Culture and Society* 28, no. 3 (2003): 801–31.

Barrett, Louise. *Beyond the Brain: How Body and Environment Shape Animal and Human Minds*. Princeton, NJ: Princeton University Press, 2011.

Basso, Keith H. "'Speaking with Names': Language and Landscape Among the Western Apache." *Cultural Anthropology* 3, no. 2 (1988): 99–130.

Beauvoir, Simone de. "Littérature et métaphysique." *Les Temps Modernes* 1, no. 7 (1946): 1153–63.

Beauvoir, Simone de. "Mon expérience d'écrivain." In *Les écrits de Simone de Beauvoir: La vie, l'écriture, avec en appendice, textes inédits ou retrouvés*. Edited by Claude Francis and Fernande Gontier, 439–57. Paris: Gallimard, 1979.

Beauvoir, Simone de. "Que peut la littérature?" *Le Monde* 249 (1965): 73–92.

Bel, Jérome. *Véronique Doisneau* (2005). https://www.jeromebel.fr/index.php?p=2&lg=2&s=8&ctid=27.

Bell, Brian G., and Jennifer Clegg. "An Ecological Approach to Reducing the Social Isolation of People with an Intellectual Disability." *Ecological Psychology* 24, no. 2 (April 30, 2012): 159–77. https://doi.org/10.1080/10407413.2012.673983.

Benjamin, Walter. "Der Flaneur." *Neue Rundschau* 78, no. 4 (1967): 549–74.

Bennett, Jane. *Vibrant Matter: A Political Ecology of Things*. Durham, NC: Duke University Press, 2010.

Benveniste, Émile. *Problems in General Linguistics*. Translated by Mary Elizabeth Meek. Miami Linguistics Series 8. Coral Gables: University of Miami Press, 1971.

Bernardin, Susan. "Intergenerational Memory and the Making of Indigenous Literary Kinships." In *Gender in American Literature and Culture*, edited by Jean M. Lutes and Jennifer Travis. 1st ed. Cambridge: Cambridge University Press, 2021. https://doi.org/10.1017/9781108763790.010.

Blu Wakpa, Tria. "From *Buffalo Dance* to Tatanka Kcizapi Wakpala, 1894–2020: Indigenous Human and More-Than-Human Choreographies of Sovereignty and Survival." *American Quarterly* 74, no. 4 (December 2022): 895–920. https://doi.org/10.1353/aq.2022.0062.

Boero, Natalie, and Katherine Mason, eds. *The Oxford Handbook of the Sociology of Body and Embodiment*. Oxford: Oxford University Press, 2021.

Bourdieu, Pierre. *Outline of a Theory of Practice*. Translated by Richard Nice. Cambridge: Cambridge University Press, 1977.

Bovet, Simon, and Rolf Pfeifer. "Emergence of Coherent Behaviors from Homogenous Sensorimotor Coupling." In *ICAR '05. Proceedings, 12th International Conference on Advanced Robotics*, 2005. https://doi.org/10.1109/ICAR.2005.1507431.

Burke, Siobhan. "Dancing Bodies That Proclaim: Black Lives Matter." *New York Times*, June 9, 2020. https://praxispace.com/wp-content/uploads/2020/06/Dancing-Bodies-That-Proclaim_-Black-Lives-Matter-The-New-York-Times.pdf.

Burkhart, Brian. *Indigenizing Philosophy Through the Land: A Trickster Methodology for Decolonizing Environmental Ethics and Indigenous Futures*. American Indian Studies Series. East Lansing: Michigan State University Press, 2019.

Burkhart, Brian. "'Locality Is a Metaphysical Fact'—Theories of Coloniality and Indigenous Liberation Through the Land: A Critical Look at *Red Skin, White Masks*." *APA Newsletter on Indigenous Philosophy* 15, no. 2 (Spring 2016): 1–6.

Butler, Judith. *Gender Trouble: Feminism and the Subversion of Identity*. London: Routledge, 1990.

Cajete, Gregory. *Native Science: Natural Laws of Interdependence*. 1st ed. Santa Fe: Clear Light Publishers, 2000.

Carolan, Michael. *Embodied Food Politics*. London: Routledge, Taylor and Francis Group, 2016.

Carter, Paul. *The Road to Botany Bay: An Exploration of Landscape and History*. Minneapolis: University of Minnesota Press, 2010.

Casey, Edward S. *The Fate of Place: A Philosophical History*. Berkeley: University of California Press, 1998.

Casey, Edward S. *Getting Back into Place: Toward a Renewed Understanding of the Place-World*. Bloomington: Indiana University Press, 1993.

Castañeda, Antonia I. "Engendering the History of Alta California, 1769–1848: Gender, Sexuality, and the Family." *California History* 76, nos. 2–3 (July 1, 1997): 230–59. https://doi.org/10.2307/25161668.

Certeau, Michel de. *The Practice of Everyday Life*. Translated by Steven Rendall. Berkeley: University of California Press, 1984.

Cervenak, Sarah Jane. *Wandering: Philosophical Performances of Racial and Sexual Freedom*. Durham, NC: Duke University Press, 2014.

Chambers, Paul Anthony. "Epistemology and Domination: Problems with the Coloniality of Knowledge Thesis in Latin American Decolonial Theory." *Dados* 63, no. 4 (2020): e20190147. https://doi.org/10.1590/dados.2020.63.4.221.

Charlson, Doria E. "Framing Black Labor: On Archives and Mine Dancing in South African Gold Mines, 1950–1970." *TDR/The Drama Review* 64, no. 3 (September 2020): 79–99. https://doi.org/10.1162/dram_a_00944.

Chemero, Anthony P. *Radical Embodied Cognitive Science*. Cambridge, MA: MIT Press, 2009.

Connerton, Paul. *How Modernity Forgets*. Cambridge: Cambridge University Press, 2009.

Connerton, Paul. *How Societies Remember*. Cambridge: Cambridge University Press, 1989.

Cornazzano, Antonio. *Libro dell'arte del danzare/Intitulato e Composto per Antonio Cornazano Alla Illustre Madonna Hippolyta, Duchessa Di Calabria*. 1455.

Csordas, Thomas. *The Body as Representation and Being-in-the-World*. Cambridge: Cambridge University Press, 1994.

D'Amato, Alison. "Movement as Matter: A Practice-Based Inquiry into the Substance of Dancing." *Dance Research Journal* 53, no. 3 (December 2021): 69–86. https://doi.org/10.1017/S0149767721000346.

Dangeli, Mique'l. "Dancing Chiax, Dancing Sovereignty: Performing Protocol in Unceded Territories." *Dance Research Journal* 48, no. 1 (April 2016): 75–90. https://doi.org/10.1017/S0149767715000534.

Daniel, Yvonne. *Dancing Wisdom: Embodied Knowledge in Haitian Vodou, Cuban Yoruba, and Bahian Candomblé*. Urbana: University of Illinois Press, 2005.

Da Pesaro, Guglielmo Ebreo. *De pratica seu arte tripudii (On the Practice or Art of Dancing)*. Edited and translated by Barbara Sparti. Oxford: Clarendon Press, 1993.

Da Piacenza, Domenico. *Fifteenth-Century Dance and Music: Twelve Transcribed Italian Treatises and Collections in the Tradition of Domenico da Piacenza*. Vol. 1: *Treatises and Music*, translated and annotated by A. William Smith. Hillsdale, NY: Pendragon Press, 1995.

De Brigard, Felipe. "Is Memory for Remembering? Recollection as a Form of Episodic

Hypothetical Thinking." *Synthese* 191, no. 2 (January 2014): 155–85. https://doi.org/10.1007/s11229-013-0247-7.

DeFrantz, Thomas F. "Breaking in My House: Popular Dance, Gender Identities, and Postracial Empathies." In *The Oxford Handbook of Hip Hop Dance Studies*, edited by Mary Fogarty, and Imani Kai Johnson. New York: Oxford, 2022.

DeFrantz, Thomas F. *Dancing Revelations: Alvin Ailey's Embodiment of African American Culture*. Oxford: Oxford University Press, 2006.

Deloria, Vine, Jr. *Spirit and Reason: The Vine Deloria, Jr., Reader*. Edited by Barbara Deloria, Kristen Foehner, and Samuel Scinta. Golden, CO: Fulcrum, 1999.

Di Paolo, Ezequiel, and Evan Thompson. "The Enactive Approach." In *The Routledge Handbook of Embodied Cognition*, edited by Lawrence Shapiro. London: Routledge, 2014.

Dijkstra, Katinka, Michael P. Kaschak, and Rolf A. Zwaan. "Body Posture Facilitates Retrieval of Autobiographical Memories." *Cognition* 102, no. 1 (January 2007): 139–49. https://doi.org/10.1016/j.cognition.2005.12.009.

Dokumaci, Arseli. "People as Affordances: Building Disability Worlds Through Care Intimacy." *Current Anthropology* 61, no. S21 (February 2020): S97–S108. https://doi.org/10.1086/705783.

Donald, Dwayne Trevor. "Forts, Curriculum, and Indigenous Métissage: Imagining Decolonization of Aboriginal-Canadian Relations in Educational Contexts." *First Nations Perspectives* 2, no. 1 (2009): 1–24.

Doti, Lynne. "Spanish California Missions: An Economic Success." *Economics Faculty Articles and Research* 213 (2019). https://digitalcommons.chapman.edu/economics_articles/213.

Duane, Daniel. "A People's History of the Sierra Nevada: Can We Celebrate Our Parks and Wilderness Areas and Still Keep in Mind the Horrors That Sometimes Happened There?" *Sierra*, June 6, 2016. https://www.sierraclub.org/sierra/2016-4-july-august/americas-national-parks/people-s-history-sierra-nevada.

Dussel, Enrique D. *The Invention of the Americas: Eclipse of "the Other" and the Myth of Modernity*. New York: Continuum, 1995.

Edelman, Gerald. *Neural Darwinism: The Theory of Neuronal Group Selection*. New York: Basic Books, 1987.

Edensor, Tim. "Walking in Rhythms: Place, Regulation, Style and the Flow of Experience." *Visual Studies* 25, no. 1 (March 23, 2010): 69–79. https://doi.org/10.1080/14725861003606902.

Erdrich, Louise. *The Painted Drum*. New York: Harper, 2005.

Fabian, Johannes. *Time and the Other: How Anthropology Makes Its Object*. New York: Columbia University Press, 2014.

Fanon, Frantz. *Black Skin, White Masks*. Translated by Richard Philcox. New York: Grove Press, 2008.

Federici, Silvia. *Caliban and the Witch: Women, the Body and Primitive Accumulation*. Brooklyn: Autonomedia, 2004.

Fend, Miriam, Hiroshi Yokoi, and Rolf Pfeifer. "Optimal Morphology of a Biologically-Inspired Whisker Array on an Obstacle-Avoiding Robot." In *Advances in Artificial*

Life, edited by Wolfgang Banzhaf, Jens Ziegler, Thomas Christaller, Peter Dittrich, and Jan T. Kim. Berlin: Springer, 2003.

Foster, Susan Leigh. *Choreographing Empathy: Kinesthesia in Performance*. New York: Routledge, 2011.

Foster, Susan Leigh. *Valuing Dance: Commodities and Gifts in Motion*. New York: Oxford University Press, 2019.

Foucault, Michel. *Discipline and Punish: The Birth of the Prison*. Translated by Alan Sheridan. New York: Pantheon Books, 1977.

Franco, Susanne, and Marina Nordera, eds. *The Oxford Handbook on Dance and Memory*. Oxford: Oxford University Press, forthcoming.

Franko, Mark. "Repeatability, Reconstruction and Beyond." *Theatre Journal* 41, no. 1 (March 1989): 56–74. https://doi.org/10.2307/3207924.

Franko, Mark. *The Dancing Body in Renaissance Choreography: Kinetic Theatricality and Social Interaction*. Rev. ed. London: Anthem, 2022.

Gamble, Christopher N., Joshua S. Hanan, and Thomas Nail. "What Is New Materialism?" *Angelaki* 24, no. 6 (November 2, 2019): 111–34. https://doi.org/10.1080/0969725X.2019.1684704.

Gani, Jasmine K., and Rabea M. Khan. "Positionality Statements as a Function of Coloniality: Interrogating Reflexive Methodologies." *International Studies Quarterly* 68, no. 2 (March 14, 2024): sqae038. https://doi.org/10.1093/isq/sqae038.

Garland-Thomson, Rosemarie. "The Case for Conserving Disability." *Journal of Bioethical Inquiry* 9, no. 3 (September 2012): 339–55. https://doi.org/10.1007/s11673-012-9380-0.

Garland-Thomson, Rosemarie. *Extraordinary Bodies: Figuring Physical Disability in American Culture and Literature*. New York: Columbia University Press, 1997.

Garroutte, Eva Marie, and Kathleen Delores Westcott. "The Story Is a Living Being: Companionship with Stories in Anishinaabeg Studies." In *Centering Anishinaabeg Studies: Understanding the World Through Stories*, edited by Jill Doerfler, Niigaanwewidam James Sinclair, and Heidi Kiiwetinepinesiik Stark. East Lansing: Michigan State University Press, 2013.

Giard, Luce. "Gesture Sequences." In *The Practice of Everyday Life*. Vol. 2, *Living and Cooking*, edited by Michel de Certeau, Luce Giard, and Pierre Mayol. Minneapolis: University of Minnesota Press, 1998.

Giard, Luce. "The Nourishing Arts." In *The Practice of Everyday Life*. Vol. 2, *Living and Cooking*, edited by Michel de Certeau, Luce Giard, and Pierre Mayol. Minneapolis: University of Minnesota Press, 1998.

Gibson, James J. *The Ecological Approach to Visual Perception*. Boston: Houghton Mifflin, 1979.

Gibson, James J. *The Senses Considered as Perceptual Systems*. Boston: Houghton Mifflin, 1966.

Glenberg, Arthur M. "What Memory Is For." *Behavioral and Brain Sciences* 20, no. 1 (March 1997): 1–19. https://doi.org/10.1017/S0140525X97000010.

Glissant, Édouard. *Caribbean Discourse: Selected Essays*. Translated by J. Michael Dash. Charlottesville: University Press of Virginia, 1989.

Glissant, Édouard. *Poetics of Relation*. Translated by Betsy Wing. Ann Arbor: University of Michigan Press, 1997.

Goeman, Mishuana. "From Place to Territories and Back Again: Centering Storied Land in the Discussion of Indigenous Nation-Building." *International Journal of Critical Indigenous Studies* 1, no. 1 (January 1, 2008): 34. https://doi.org/10.5204/ijcis.v1i1.20.

Goeman, Mishuana. "(Re)Mapping Indigenous Presence on the Land in Native Women's Literature." *American Quarterly* 60, no. 2 (June 2008): 295–302. https://doi.org/10.1353/aq.0.0011.

Gooch, Pernille. "Feet Following Hooves." In *Ways of Walking: Ethnography and Practice on Foot*, edited by Tim Ingold and Jo Lee Verguns, 67–80t. Aldershot, UK: Ashgate, 2008.

Gottschild, Brenda Dixon. *Digging the Africanist Presence in Contemporary Performance: Dance and Other Contexts*. Westport, CT: Praeger, 1996.

Gros, Frédéric. *A Philosophy of Walking*. Translated by John Howe. London: Verso, 2015.

Grosfoguel, Ramón. "The Structure of Knowledge in Westernized Universities: Epistemic Racism/Sexism and the Four Genocides/Epistemicides of the Long 16th Century." *Human Architecture: Journal of the Sociology of Self-Knowledge* 11, no. 1 (2013): 73–90.

Grosz, Elizabeth. *Volatile Bodies: Toward a Corporeal Feminism*. Bloomington: Indiana University Press, 1994.

Halberstam, Judith. *Female Masculinity*. Durham, NC: Duke University Press, 1998.

Hammergren, Lena. "The Re-Turn of the Flâneuse." In *Corporealities: Dancing, Knowledge, Culture and Power*, edited by Susan Leigh Foster. London: Routledge, 1996.

Haraway, Donna. "Situated Knowledges: The Science Question in Feminism and the Privilege of Partial Perspective." *Feminist Studies* 14, no. 3 (1988): 575–99. https://doi.org/10.2307/3178066.

Harding, Sandra G. *The Science Question in Feminism*. Ithaca, NY: Cornell University Press, 1986.

Harjo, Laura. *Spiral to the Stars: Mvskoke Tools of Futurity*. Critical Issues in Indigenous Studies. Tucson: University of Arizona Press, 2019.

Hau'ofa, Epeli. "Our Sea of Islands." *Contemporary Pacific* 6, no. 1 (1994): 148–61.

Hawkesworth, Mary. *Embodied Power: Demystifying Disembodied Politics*. London: Routledge, 2016.

Heyes, Cecilia, and Caroline Catmur. "What Happened to Mirror Neurons?" *Perspectives on Psychological Science* 17, no. 1 (January 2022): 153–68. https://doi.org/10.1177/1745691621990638.

Hill Collins, Patricia. *Black Feminist Thought: Knowledge, Consciousness, and the Politics of Empowerment*. London: Routledge, 2000.

Hodson, Millicent, Kenneth Archer, and Shira Klasmer. *The Lost Rite: Rediscovery of the 1913 Rite of Spring*. 2nd ed. London: KMS Press, 2016.

Hokowhitu, Brendan. "Indigenous Existentialism and the Body." *Cultural Studies Review* 15, no. 2 (September 2009): 101–18. https://doi.org/10.7939/R3BZ6174C.

Husserl, Edmund. "The World of the Living Present and the Constitution of the Surrounding World External to the Organism." In *Husserl: Shorter Works*, edited by Peter

McCormick and Frederick A. Elliston. Notre Dame, IN: University of Notre Dame Press, 1981.

Hyslop, Stephen G. *Contest for California: From Spanish Colonization to the American Conquest. Before Gold: California Under Spain and Mexico*, Vol. 2. Norman, OK: Arthur H. Clark, 2012.

Ingold, Tim. "Culture on the Ground: The World Perceived Through the Feet." *Journal of Material Culture* 9, no. 3 (November 2004): 315–40. https://doi.org/10.1177/1359183504046896.

Ingold, Tim. "Footprints Through the Weather-World: Walking, Breathing, Knowing." *Journal of the Royal Anthropological Institute* 16, no. S1 (May 2010): S121–S139. https://doi.org/10.1111/j.1467-9655.2010.01613.x.

Ingold, Tim. "Walking the Plank: Meditations on a Process of Skill." In *Defining Technological Literacy: Towards an Epistemological Framework*, edited by John R. Dakers. New York: Palgrave Macmillan, 2006.

Ingold, Tim, and Jo Lee Vergunst, eds. *Ways of Walking: Ethnography and Practice on Foot*. Aldershot, UK: Ashgate, 2008.

Johnson, Imani Kai. *Dark Matter in Breaking Cyphers: The Life of Africanist Aesthetics in Global Hip Hop*. New York: Oxford University Press, 2023.

Jones, Amelia. "Material Traces: Performativity, Artistic 'Work,' and New Concepts of Agency." TDR/*The Drama Review* 59, no. 4 (December 2015): 18–35. https://doi.org/10.1162/DRAM_a_00494.

Kim, Jina B. "Toward a Crip-of-Color Critique: Thinking with Minich's 'Enabling Whom?'" *Lateral* 6, no. 1 (May 2017). https://doi.org/10.25158/L6.1.14.

Kimmerer, Robin Wall. *Braiding Sweetgrass: Indigenous Wisdom, Scientific Knowledge, and the Teachings of Plants*. Minneapolis: Milkweed Editions, 2013.

King, Tiffany Lethabo. *The Black Shoals: Offshore Formations of Black and Native Studies*. Durham, NC: Duke University Press, 2019.

Kirby, Vicki. *Telling Flesh: The Substance of the Corporeal*. New York: Routledge, 1997.

Kirkman, George W. *The Kirkman-Harriman Pictorial and Historical Map of Los Angeles County, A.D. 1860*. SCV Historical Society, accessed May 8, 2024. https://scvhistory.com/scvhistory/la3701.htm.

Krokos, Eric, Catherine Plaisant, and Amitabh Varshney. "Virtual Memory Palaces: Immersion Aids Recall." *Virtual Reality* 23, no. 1 (March 5, 2019): 1–15. https://doi.org/10.1007/s10055-018-0346-3.

Kyselo, Miriam, and Ezequiel Di Paolo. "Locked-in Syndrome: A Challenge for Embodied Cognitive Science." *Phenomenlogy and the Cognitive Sciences* 14 (2015): 517–42. https://doi.org/10.1007/s11097-013-9344-9.

Lakoff, George, and Mark Johnson. *Philosophy in the Flesh: The Embodied Mind and Its Challenge to Western Thought*. New York: Basic Books, 1999.

Landy, David, and Robert L. Goldstone. "Proximity and Precedence in Arithmetic." *Quarterly Journal of Experimental Psychology* 63, no. 10 (October 2010): 1953–68. https://doi.org/10.1080/17470211003787619.

Laurenti, Jean-Noël. "Feuillet's Thinking." In *Traces of Dance: Drawings and Notations of Choreographers*, edited by Laurence Louppe. Paris: Editions Dis Voir, 1994.

Lee, C. C. "On with the Dance." UCLA *Magazine*, Spring 2003.

Lefebvre, Henri. *The Production of Space*. Translated by Donald Nicholson-Smith. Oxford: Blackwell Publishing, 1991.

Legat, Allice. *Walking the Land, Feeding the Fire: Knowledge and Stewardship Among the Tłı̨chǫ Dene*. Tucson: University of Arizona Press, 2012.

Lepecki, André, ed. *Of the Presence of the Body: Essays on Dance and Performance Theory*. Middletown, CT: Wesleyan University Press, 2004.

Lepecki, André. *Exhausting Dance: Performance and the Politics of Movement*. New York: Routledge, 2006.

Liboiron, Max. *Pollution Is Colonialism*. Durham, NC: Duke University Press, 2021.

Lightfoot, Kent G. *Indians, Missionaries, and Merchants: The Legacy of Colonial Encounters on the California Frontiers*. Berkeley: University of California Press, 2006.

Little Bear, Leroy. "Traditional Knowledge and Humanities: A Perspective by a Blackfoot." *Journal of Chinese Philosophy* 39, no. 4 (December 2012): 518–27. https://doi.org/10.1111/j.1540-6253.2012.01742.x.

Lovern, Lavonna. "Native American Worldview and the Discourse on Disability." *Essays in Philosophy* 9, no. 1 (2008): 113–20. https://doi.org/10.5840/eip20089123.

Lovern, Lavonna L. "Indigenous Perspectives on Difference: A Case for Inclusion." *Journal of Literary and Cultural Disability Studies* 11, no. 3 (August 2017): 303–20. https://doi.org/10.3828/jlcds.2017.24.

Martin, Randy. *Critical Moves: Dance Studies in Theory and Politics*. Durham, NC: Duke University Press, 1998.

Martin, Randy. "Dance as a Social Movement." *Social Text*, no. 12 (1985): 54–70. https://doi.org/10.2307/466604.

Martin, Randy. "A Precarious Dance, a Derivative Sociality." TDR/*The Drama Review* 56, no. 4 (Dec. 2012), 62–77. doi: https://doi.org/10.1162/DRAM_a_00214.

Mason, William Marvin. "Fages' Code of Conduct Toward Indians, 1787." *Journal of California Anthropology* 2, no. 1 (1975). https://escholarship.org/uc/item/3pd0064b.

Mauss, Marcel. "Techniques of the Body." *Economy and Society* 2, no. 1 (1973): 70–88.

McBeth, Sally. "Memory, History, and Contested Pasts: Re-Imagining Sacagawea/Sacajawea." *American Indian Culture and Research Journal* 27, no. 1 (2003). https://www.unco.edu/hss/anthropology/pdf/mcbeth/reimagining-sacagawea.pdf.

McDonough, Tom. "The Crimes of the Flaneur." *October* 102 (Fall 2002): 101–22.

McFee, Graham. *Understanding Dance*. London: Routledge, 1992.

Meagher, Sharon M. "Philosophy in the Streets: Walking the City with Engels and de Certeau." *City* 11, no. 1 (April 2007): 7–20. https://doi.org/10.1080/13604810701200722.

Merleau-Ponty, Maurice. *Phenomenology of Perception*. Translated by Colin Smith. London: Routledge and Kegan Paul, 1962.

Merleau-Ponty, Maurice. *The Visible and the Invisible*. Translated by Alphonso Lingis. Evanston, IL: Northwestern University Press, 1968.

Merritt, Michele. "Thinking-Is-Moving: Dance, Agency, and a Radically Enactive Mind." *Phenomenology and the Cognitive Sciences* 14, no. 1 (March 2015): 95–110. https://doi.org/10.1007/s11097-013-9314-2.

Middleton, Jennie. "Sense and the City: Exploring the Embodied Geographies of Urban Walking." *Social and Cultural Geography* 11, no. 6 (September 2010): 575–96. https://doi.org/10.1080/14649365.2010.497913.

Midge, Tiffany. "Thousands of Jingle Dress Dancers Appear at Standing Rock." ICT, November 7, 2016. https://ictnews.org/archive/thousands-of-jingle-dress-dancers-appear-at-standing-rock.

Migdalek, Jack. *The Embodied Performance of Gender*. London: Routledge, 2014.

Mignolo, Walter D. *The Darker Side of the Renaissance: Literacy, Territoriality, and Colonization*. Ann Arbor: University of Michigan Press, 1995.

Minich, Julie Avril. "Enabling Whom? Critical Disability Studies Now." *Lateral* 5, no. 1 (May 2016). https://doi.org/10.25158/L5.1.9.

Miranda, Deborah A. "'Saying the Padre Had Grabbed Her': Rape Is the Weapon, Story Is the Cure." *Intertexts* 14, no. 2 (September 2010): 93–112. https://doi.org/10.1353/itx.2011.0005.

Mitchell, Sam, and Julie Burelle. "*Dee(a)r Spine*: Dance, Dramaturgy, and the Repatriation of Indigenous Memory." *Dance Research Journal* 48, no. 1 (2016): 41–54. https://doi.org/10.1017/S0149767715000546.

Moreton-Robinson, Aileen. "Relationality: A Key Presupposition of an Indigenous Social Research Paradigm." In *Sources and Methods in Indigenous Studies*, edited by Chris Andersen and Jean M. O'Brien. London: Routledge, 2017. https://cat.lib.unimelb.edu.au:443/record=b8787578~S30.

Moreton-Robinson, Aileen. "Towards an Australian Indigenous Women's Standpoint Theory: A Methodological Tool." *Australian Feminist Studies* 28, no. 78 (December 2013): 331–47. https://doi.org/10.1080/08164649.2013.876664.

Ness, Sally Ann. "Dancing in the Field: Notes from Memory." In *Corporealities: Dancing, Knowledge, Culture and Power*, edited by Susan Leigh Foster. London: Routledge, 1996.

Noudelmann, François. "Literature: The Archipelago Perspective." *Interdisciplinary Literary Studies* 20, no. 2 (June 15, 2018): 203–16. https://doi.org/10.5325/intelitestud.20.2.0203.

Novack, Cynthia Jean. *Sharing the Dance: Contact Improvisation and American Culture*. New Directions in Anthropological Writing. Madison: University of Wisconsin Press, 1990.

Pearce, Margaret W. "Encroachment by Word, Axis, and Tree: Mapping Techniques from the Colonization of New England." *Cartographic Perspectives*, no. 48 (June 1, 2004): 24–38. https://doi.org/10.14714/CP48.457.

Peeters, Anco, and Miguel Segundo-Ortin. "Misplacing Memories? An Enactive Approach to the Virtual Memory Palace." *Consciousness and Cognition* 76 (November 2019): 102834. https://doi.org/10.1016/j.concog.2019.102834.

Pfeifer, Rolf, and Josh Bongard. *How the Body Shapes the Way We Think: A New View of Intelligence*. Cambridge, MA: MIT Press, 2007.

Phelan, Peggy. *Unmarked: The Politics of Performance*. London: Routledge, 1996.

Porter, Lindsey Archer. "The Domestic Stage: Dance and Intimacy in the Age of New

Media." PhD diss., University of California, Los Angeles, 2022. https://escholarship
.org/uc/item/4sh3f8td.

Recollet, Karyn. "Gesturing Indigenous Futurities Through the Remix." *Dance Research Journal* 48, no. 1 (April 2016): 91–105. https://doi.org/10.1017/S0149767715000492.

Rifkin, Mark. *Beyond Settler Time: Temporal Sovereignty and Indigenous Self-Determination.* Durham, NC: Duke University Press, 2017.

Rosa, Cristina F. *Brazilian Bodies and Their Choreographies of Identification: Swing Nation.* London: Palgrave Macmillan, 2015.

Rosenfield, Israel. *The Invention of Memory: A New View of the Brain.* New York: Basic Books, 1988.

Rosiek, Jerry Lee, Jimmy Snyder, and Scott L. Pratt. "The New Materialisms and Indigenous Theories of Non-Human Agency: Making the Case for Respectful Anti-Colonial Engagement." *Qualitative Inquiry* 26, nos. 3–4 (March 2020): 331–46. https://doi.org/10.1177/1077800419830135.

Roy, Arundhati. "The Pandemic Is a Portal." *Financial Times*, April 3, 2020.

Said, Edward W. *Orientalism.* New York: Vintage Books, 1979.

Santos, Boaventura de Sousa. *Epistemologies of the South: Justice Against Epistemicide.* London: Routledge, 2014.

Seamon, David. "Body-Subject, Time-Space Routines, and Place-Ballets." In *The Human Experience of Space and Place*, edited by Anne Buttimer and David Seamon. London: Routledge, 1980.

Seamon, David. *A Geography of the Lifeworld: Movement, Rest and Encounter.* London: Croom Helm, 1979.

Sedgwick, Eve Kosofsky. *Epistemology of the Closet.* Berkeley: University of California Press, 1990.

Sekimoto, Sachi, and Christopher Brown. *Race and the Senses: The Felt Politics of Racial Embodiment.* New York: Routledge, 2020.

Sepulveda, Charles. "Our Sacred Waters: Theorizing Kuuyam as a Decolonial Possibility." *Decolonization: Indigeneity, Education, and Society* 7, no. 1 (2018): 40–58.

Sharpe, Christina Elizabeth. *In the Wake: On Blackness and Being.* Durham, NC: Duke University Press, 2016.

Shea Murphy, Jacqueline. *Dancing Indigenous Worlds: Choreographies of Relation.* Minneapolis: University of Minnesota Press, 2022.

Shea Murphy, Jacqueline. *The People Have Never Stopped Dancing: Native American Modern Dance Histories.* Minneapolis: University of Minnesota Press, 2007.

Sheets-Johnstone, Maxine. "Emotion and Movement: A Beginning Empirical-Phenomenological Analysis of Their Relationship." *Journal of Consciousness Studies* 6, nos. 11–12 (January 1, 1999): 259–77.

Sheets-Johnstone, Maxine. "Kinesthetic Memory." *Theoria et Historia Scientiarum* 7, no. 1 (January 2, 2007): 69–92. https://doi.org/10.12775/ths.2003.005.

Shehadeh, Raja. *Palestinian Walks: Notes on a Vanishing Landscape.* London: Profile Books, 2007.

Shildrick, Margrit. *Embodying the Monster: Encounters with the Vulnerable Self.* London: SAGE Publications, 2002.

Simpson, Leanne Betasamosake. *As We Have Always Done: Indigenous Freedom Through Radical Resistance*. Minneapolis: University of Minnesota Press, 2017.

Simpson, Leanne Betasamosake. "Land as Pedagogy: Nishnaabeg Intelligence and Rebellious Transformation." *Decolonization: Indigeneity, Education and Society* 3, no. 3 (2014): 1–25.

Sobchack, Vivian. "'Choreography for One, Two, and Three Legs' (A Phenomenological Meditation in Movements)." *Topoi* 24, no. 1 (January 2005): 55–66. https://doi.org/10.1007/s11245-004-4161-y.

Solnit, Rebecca. *Wanderlust: A History of Walking*. London: Penguin Books, 2001.

Stuckey, Sterling. *Slave Culture: Nationalist Theory and the Foundations of Black America*, 25th anniversary edition. New York: Oxford University Press, 2013.

Styres, Sandra, Celia Haig-Brown, and Melissa Blimkie. "Toward a Pedagogy of Land: The Urban Context." *Canadian Journal of Education/Revue canadienne de l éducation* 36, no. 2 (2013): 188–221.

Sweet, Jill. *Dances of the Tewa Pueblo Indians: Expressions of New Life*. 2nd ed. Santa Fe: School of American Research Press, 2004.

Tapias, Maria. *Embodied Protests: Emotions and Women's Health in Bolivia*. Urbana: University of Illinois Press, 2015.

Taylor, Diana. *The Archive and the Repertoire: Performing Cultural Memory in the Americas*. Durham, NC: Duke University Press, 2003.

Thanem, Torkild, and David Knights. *Embodied Research Methods*. London: SAGE Publications, 2019.

Thompson, Evan. *Mind in Life: Biology, Phenomenology, and the Sciences of Mind*. Cambridge, MA: Harvard University Press, 2007.

Tinker, George E. "The Stones Shall Cry Out: Consciousness, Rocks, and Indians." *Wicazo Sa Review* 19, no. 2 (2004): 105–25. https://doi.org/10.1353/wic.2004.0027.

Tuck, Eve, Marcia McKenzie, and Kate McCoy. "Introduction—Land Education: Indigenous, Post-Colonial, and Decolonizing Perspectives on Place and Environmental Education Research." In *Land Education: Rethinking Pedagogies of Place from Indigenous, Postcolonial, and Decolonizing Perspectives*, edited by Kate McCoy, Eve Tuck, and Marcia McKenzie. London: Routledge, 2016.

Tuck, Eve, and K. Wayne Yang. "Decolonization Is Not a Metaphor." *Decolonization: Indigeneity, Education and Society* 1, no. 1 (2012): 1–40.

Tuck-Po, Lye. "Before a Step Too Far: Walking with Batek Hunter-Gatherers in the Forests of Pahang, Malaysia." In *Ways of Walking: Ethnography and Practice on Foot*, edited by Tim Ingold and Jo Lee Vergunst. Aldershot, UK: Ashgate, 2008.

Turocy, Catherine. "Taught by Pygmalion." The Historical Dance Society Lectures, August 18, 2021. https://www.youtube.com/watch?v=GIGiOxaeV-E.

Tynan, Lauren. "What Is Relationality? Indigenous Knowledges, Practices and Responsibilities with Kin." *Cultural Geographies* 28, no. 4 (October 2021): 597–610. https://doi.org/10.1177/14744740211029287.

UCLA. "Our Story Maps." Mapping Indigenous LA. Accessed January 2, 2025. https://

www.bing.com/search?pc=MOZI&form=MOZLBR&q=UCLA%2C+Mapping
+Indigenous+LA%2C+%E2%80%9CVisit+Our+Story+Maps.%E2%80%9D+.

Van Dooren, Thom, and Deborah Bird Rose. "Storied-Places in a Multispecies City." *Humanimalia* 3, no. 2 (February 12, 2012): 1–27. https://doi.org/10.52537/humanimalia.10046.

Vergunst, Jo Lee. "Taking a Trip and Taking Care in Everyday Life." In *Ways of Walking: Ethnography and Practice on Foot*, edited by Tim Ingold and Jo Lee Vergunst. Aldershot, UK: Ashgate, 2008.

Wacquant, Loïc. "For a Sociology of Flesh and Blood." *Qualitative Sociology* 38, no. 1 (March 2015): 1–11. https://doi.org/10.1007/s11133-014-9291-y.

Ward, Julia. "A Course in Miracles: Avila, like the Phoenix, Rises (With a Little Help from King and a Few Other Friends)." The Dance Insider, accessed April 9, 2024. http://www.danceinsider.com/f2002/f0813_1.html.

Watts Belser, Julia. "Vital Wheels: Disability, Relationality, and the Queer Animacy of Vibrant Things." *Hypatia* 31, no. 1 (2016): 5–21. https://doi.org/10.1111/hypa.12217.

Watts, Vanessa. "Indigenous Place-Thought and Agency Amongst Humans and Non Humans (First Woman and Sky Woman Go on a European World Tour!)." *Decolonization: Indigeneity, Education and Society* 2, no. 1 (2013): 20–34.

Weighill, Tharon. "The 2-Step Tales of Hahashka: Experiences in Corporeality and Embodiment in Aboriginal California." PhD diss., University of California, Riverside, 2004.

Welch, Rosanne. "A Brief History of the Tongva Tribe: The Native Inhabitants of the Lands of the Puente Hills Preserve." PhD diss., Claremont Graduate University, 2006.

Wiedorn, Michael. "On the Unfolding of Édouard Glissant's Archipelagic Thought." *Karib—Nordic Journal for Caribbean Studies* 6, no. 1 (February 26, 2021): 3. https://doi.org/10.16993/karib.82.

Wilson, Margaret. "The Case for Sensorimotor Coding in Working Memory." *Psychonomic Bulletin and Review* 8, no. 1 (March 2001): 44–57. https://doi.org/10.3758/BF03196138.

Wilson, Shawn. *Research Is Ceremony: Indigenous Research Methods*. Black Point, NS: Fernwood Publishing, 2008.

Wunderlich, Filipa Matos. "Walking and Rhythmicity: Sensing Urban Space." *Journal of Urban Design* 13, no. 1 (February 2008): 125–39. https://doi.org/10.1080/13574800701803472.

Wylie, John. "A Single Day's Walking: Narrating Self and Landscape on the South West Coast Path." *Transactions of the Institute of British Geographers* 30, no. 2 (June 2005): 234–47. https://doi.org/10.1111/j.1475-5661.2005.00163.x.

Wynter, Sylvia. "1492: New World View." In *Race, Discourse, and the Origin of the Americas: A New World View*, edited by Vera Lawrence and Rex Nettleford. Washington, DC: Smithsonian Institution Press, 1995.

Wynter, Sylvia. "Beyond the Categories of the Master Conception: The Counterdoctrine of the Jamesian Poiesis." In *C. L. R. James's Caribbean*, edited by Paget Henry and Paul Buhle. Durham, NC: Duke University Press, 1992.

Wynter, Sylvia. "Beyond the Word of Man: Glissant and the New Discourse of the Antilles." *World Literature Today* 63, no. 4 (1989): 637–48. https://doi.org/10.2307/40145557.

Wynter, Sylvia. "Unsettling the Coloniality of Being/Power/Truth/Freedom: Towards the Human, After Man, Its Overrepresentation—An Argument." cr: *The New Centennial Review* 3, no. 3 (2003): 257–337.

Yates, Frances A. *The Art of Memory*. London: Bodley Head, 2014.

Young, Iris Marion. "Throwing like a Girl: A Phenomenology of Feminine Body Comportment Motility and Spatiality." *Human Studies* 3, no. 2 (1980): 137–56.

INDEX

able-bodiedness, 16–18, 21, 112
ableism, 100–101
Absolon, Kathleen E., 130n25
Academy, the, 6, 80, 95–96, 125n17
Acjachemen people, 9, 123n1
acting, 33, 38, 65, 87; and being/knowing, 36–55; and ethics, 9, 38, 48–55; gendered, 22; and perceiving, 80, 111; and thinking, 60
affordances, 32, 34, 36, 41–43, 45, 67, 72, 128n35, 136n4; and dance, 10, 88, 97–120; definition, 17–19; gendered, 21–22; and habitus, 127n28; and memory, 84–85; racialized, 23, 128n35; and thinking, 81; and walking, 14, 19–20, 23–25, 28–29, 31, 35
Africa, 50, 63, 73–74, 134n40. *See also individual countries*
African Americans, 23
Africanist diasporic aesthetics, 66, 103, 115, 137n19
African people, 50, 74, 134n40
Afrofuturism, 125n30
Ahmed, Sara, 33, 57
Alaimo, Stacy, 7
Americas, 49–50, 59, 73–74. *See also individual countries and states*
Ancient Greece, 83, 95
Anderson, Michael, 17, 21, 61, 72, 81, 88, 115, 135n6
Anglo people, 64
Anishinaabe people, 7, 31
anthropology, 9, 57
Aotearoa Māori people, 119
Apache people, 126n9. *See also* Western Apache people

Aquinas, Thomas, 84
Arabs, 49, 73–74
Archer, Kenneth, 136n28
archipelagic thinking, 8
archipelago as method, 8–12
archive (Taylor), 60
archives, 5, 44; archiving dancing, 87–93; and memory, 10, 94–95; vs. repertoire, 60
Asia: East, 88; South, 11, 88
Asian Americans, 16, 22, 24, 101
attention/attentiveness, 30, 39, 43–44, 70, 74–75, 111–15, 135n9; and coalitional politics, 11; and connectedness, 4; dance enabling, 3, 80, 89, 102, 107–8; and embodied practice, 60–61; and knowing, 45, 68; and patience, 48, 53–54; and walking, 13–14, 20, 25–26, 29, 32
Australia, 3, 27, 31, 53, 68, 134n45
authoritarianism, 5, 11
autoethnography, 9
autonomy, 26, 37, 40, 43, 48, 50, 68, 75, 101
Avila, Homer, 100, 102, 112, 114, 136n6
AXIS Dance Company, 97
Aztec people, 73

Baggs, Edward, 61, 88, 130n30, 135n6
Bahian Candomblé, 63
ballet, 88, 92, 97, 103, 112, 115, 136n28
ballroom dance, 102, 116
Barad, Karen, 36–37, 39–43, 46–47, 52–53, 68, 123n2
baroque performances, 92, 136n28
Barrett, Louise, 17, 81
Basso, Keith, 53, 79

Beauvoir, Simone de, 57
Beaver Hills Cree people, 123n2
being, 11, 30–31, 101, 128n48, 131n37; and acting/knowing, 9, 22, 36–55; and colonialism, 2; and connectedness, 4; and dancing, 65–68, 102, 104, 110, 113, 116–17, 120; and Land, 28–29, 75; and locality, 36, 129n2; more-than-human beings, 7, 11, 22, 94; and walking, 29–30, 98. *See also* Ceremonial Beings; ontology
Bell, Brian, 100
Bennett, Jane, 68, 105
Benveniste, Émile, 34
Bharatanatyam, 88, 110
Black Americans, 125n27
Black Briton people, 97, 137n18
Blackfoot people, 130n32
Black Lives Matter, 118–19
Black people, 22, 23–24, 63, 66, 74, 97, 125n27, 127n34, 134n42, 137n18
Black South Africans, 118
Blimkie, Melissa, 125n28
Blu Wakpa, Tria, 118
bodily intelligence, 20, 109
bodily knowledge, 1
body schema, 56, 132
Bohr, Niels, 46
Bongard, Josh, 78, 82, 86, 91
boots, 27, 50, 76
botany, 47
Botany Bay, 134n45
Bourdieu, Pierre, 42, 62, 127n28
Bovet, Simon, 82
braiding, 123n2
Brazil, 66
Brazilian people, 63–64, 109
break dance, 116
Brown, Christopher, 22, 128n35
Brown, Joel, 97
Burkhart, Brian, 36–37, 39, 45–46, 49, 51, 124n8, 125n22, 125n29, 129nn2–4, 130n21, 131n36, 131n42, 134n47

Cajete, Gregory, 28, 30
California, 7, 36, 57–58, 65, 67, 95, 99, 122, 123n2; Long Beach, 15; Los Angeles city, 15, 126n4; Los Angeles County, 16; missions in, 15–16, 26, 64, 95; Ojai, 9, 126n4; Southern, 29, 134n44; Ventura County, 15
Canada, 3, 97, 100, 125n28, 128n54; Toronto, 94
capitalism, 12, 21, 37, 42, 101
capoeira Angola, 63
Caribbean, 50, 63, 66, 73, 109. *See also individual countries*
Carmel Mission, 95
Carnival, 116
Carter, Paul, 27, 128n42, 134n45
Cartesian dualism, 1, 3, 9, 11, 52, 56, 59, 91, 110, 123n5, 132; and colonialism, 2, 5, 50, 73, 75–77, 91, 96, 131n39
Casey, Edward, 27–28, 32–34, 36–37, 40–41, 126n1, 128n42
Ceremonial Beings, 94
ceremonial dance, 15, 64–65, 110
Certeau, Michel de, 9, 26
Cervenak, Sarah Jane, 23
Chain of Being, 131n39
chairs, 21, 51
Chambers, Paul Anthony, 123n5
chaparral, 13, 28, 121
Charleston (dance), 104
Chemero, Anthony, 36–37, 42, 52, 111–12, 115, 130n30
Cherokee people, 31, 36, 124n8
China, 84
Chinese opera, 88
Chippewa people, 36
Choctaw people, 136n30
choreography, 63, 65, 88–89, 110, 116–17
Christianity, 15, 49–50, 73, 75, 84, 131n39
Chumash Land, 14–15, 121, 126n4
Chumash people, 9, 65, 95
Cicero, Marcus Tullius, 83
Clark, William, 94
Clegg, Jennifer, 100
coalitional politics, 11
co-creativity, 31
Cody, Buffalo Bill, 65, 118
cognition, 27, 37, 80–81, 84, 86, 123n5, 127n19; Cartesian theories of, 75; and dance, 6, 10, 96; embodied, 57–58, 132; social, 56, 132
cognitive science, 17, 37, 58, 72, 91, 93; ecological, 2, 9–11, 57, 80–81, 84, 105, 135n6; enactivist, 57, 80, 123n4
Colombia, 123n5

154 · Index

colonialism/imperialism, 37, 124nn7–8, 125n29, 125n30, 127n24, 131n42; and archipelago as method, 8; and archives, 60; and being, 2; British, 134n45; and Cartesian dualism, 2, 5, 50, 73, 75–77, 91, 96, 131n39; and cognitive science, 11; colonizer guilt, 16; and dance, 65, 95–96, 104–11, 113, 118, 125n17; and disability, 101; and enclosure, 26–27; and knowing, 64; and Land, 28–30; neo-imperialism, 2; settler colonialism, 2, 5, 16, 28–29, 43–44, 49, 51, 58–59, 65, 95, 126n9; settler emplacement, 16; Spanish, 14–15, 26, 49–50, 65, 73, 126n4, 131n39; and walking, 9, 14–16. *See also* decoloniality; settler-scholars

Columbia University's Teaching College, 96

Columbus, Christopher, 74–75, 106

Comanche people, 94–95, 136n32

concert dance, 1, 63, 110, 117

concorporeality, 36

connectedness, 2, 6, 31, 32, 56, 76, 83–84, 99, 122, 131n37; and affordances, 10; and archipelago as method, 8; and being/knowing/acting, 9, 36–53; and dance, 3, 61, 63, 66–67, 88, 93–95, 96, 102, 104–7, 112–13, 116, 119–20; definition, 3–4, 123n2, 124n11; and Land, 45, 92, 125n28; and memory, 22; and perceiving, 10–11, 35, 80; and place, 27–28; and place-thought, 36; vs. relationality, 123n2; and walking, 9, 12–19

Connecticut, 53, 134n44

Connerton, Paul, 78, 87, 91

conquest, 15, 49, 59, 73–77, 106, 131n39

Cornazzano, Antonio, 106

COVID-19 pandemic, 11–12, 24

Cowan, Suzanne, 97

coyote discourse, 7

Cree people, 31. *See also* Beaver Hills Cree people; Opaskwayak Cree people; Plains Cree people

crip-of-color critique, 101

critical race studies, 58

Csordas, Thomas, 57

Cuban Yoruba, 63

cultural studies, 58

dance, 28, 35, 44, 54–55, 58, 60, 62, 126n9, 128n33, 137n20, 138n43; and affordances, 10, 88, 97–120; and attention/attentiveness, 3, 80, 89, 102, 107–8; and cognition, 6, 10, 96; and colonialism, 65, 95–96, 104–11, 113, 118, 125n17; and connectedness, 3, 61, 63, 66–67, 88, 93–95, 96, 102, 104–7, 112–13, 116, 119–20; and decoloniality, 93–96, 104–11; and facts, 66, 93, 98, 104, 113, 120; and knowing, 1–2, 5, 63–68, 78–80, 90–95, 98, 104–6, 112–20; and memory, 10, 78–96, 117; racialized, 23; as research, 5; as thinking, 123n4. *See also individual styles/traditions*

dance education, 1, 63, 95–96

dance history, 95

dance manuals, 106

dance notation, 92–93, 137n29, 138n33

dance pedagogies, 95–96, 105–10, 113

dance programs, 96

dance reconstruction, 92–93, 136n28

dance science, 107

dance studies, 80, 125n17

Dangeli, Mique'l, 92, 94

Daniel Yvonne, 63

Da Pesaro, Guglielmo Ebreo, 106

da Piacenza, Domenico, 106

De Brigard, Felipe, 85–86, 93

decoloniality, 8, 31; and Cartesianism, 11, 123n5; and dance, 93–96, 104–11; embodying, 9–10, 56–77; and knowing, 59, 80; and land repatriation, 2, 124n7; and memory, 93–96

decolonial studies, 2, 49, 58

deictics, 32–35

Deloria, Vine, Jr., 36–37, 46–49, 51–52, 123n2, 137n16

Descartes, René, 5, 75, 123n5. *See also* Cartesian dualism

Dewey, John, 96, 136n36

differently abled bodies, 20–21, 99, 116

Dijkstra, Katinka, 83, 128n51

Di Paolo, Ezequiel, 56, 58, 132, 135n9

dirt, 7, 17, 25, 122

disability, 24, 127n23; and affordances, 20, 100–101, 111; conserving, 138n30; and dance, 98, 103, 112; as different ability, 10, 20–21, 99, 127n23

disability studies, 2, 10–11, 57, 101

Index · 155

discipline, 1, 26, 40, 75, 90, 127n28
disco, 104
disembodiment, 9–10, 56, 59, 72–73, 132
displacement, 39, 50, 64
disorientation. *See* orientation
documentations, 90
Dokumaci, Arseli, 100
Donald, Dwayne, 123n2
Dussel, Enrique, 2, 49–50, 73, 75, 131n39

earbuds, 29, 128n48
Eastern Sierra, 9, 16, 126n4
ecological cognitive science, 2, 9–11, 57, 80–81, 84, 105, 135n6
Edelman, Gerald, 85
Edison, Thomas, 118
ego cogito, 50–51, 75
ego conquiro, 49–51
ego constituo, 51, 131n42
Electric Slide, 119
embodied cognition, 57–58
embodied knowledge, 62–68
embodied practice, 59–62
embodied scholarship, 68–72
emplacement, 13, 16, 33–34
enactivist cognitive science, 57, 80, 123n4
enclosure, 9, 26–27, 128n43, 134n44
England, 50. *See also* Great Britain; United Kingdom
English people, 125n28
ensoulment, 28
entanglement, 22, 28, 36, 39–41, 52, 64, 74
ephemerality, 39, 76, 113, 138n33
episteme, 50, 68, 73, 77, 125n29
epistemicides, 49, 73
epistemic justice, 2
epistemology, 1, 11, 44–45, 48, 51, 101, 123n5, 127n24, 131n37. *See also* knowing
Erdrich, Louise, 36, 39
essaying, 7–8
Esselen people, 95
ethics, 7, 38, 131n37, 131n45, 131nn36–37; and acting, 9, 38, 48–55
ethnicity, 22, 63, 124n8
Eurocentrism, 106
Europe, 50, 95, 131, 131n39
extractivism, 2, 5, 7, 38, 50, 75

Fabian, Johannes, 30
facts, 3, 11, 51, 60; and connectedness, 38, 49; and dance, 66, 93, 98, 104, 113, 120; and knowing, 44, 46–47, 62; and memory, 78–79, 84–85, 87, 89
Fages, Pedro, 126n9
Fages's Code of Conduct, 126n9
feet, 17, 27, 50, 54, 66, 98, 111–12
femininity, 6, 22, 43
feminism, 7, 14, 57, 123n5
Ferdinand II (king), 75
Fiji, 8
Filipinas, 118
First Nations, 92, 131n37. *See also individual nations*
Fitbit, 44
flaneurs/flaneuses, 23, 127n31
flesh (Merleau-Ponty), 36, 41
Foucault, Michel, 40, 73, 127n28
France, 50, 137n29; Illiers, 83
French people, 125n28

Garcia, Andy, 66
Garland-Thomson, Rosemarie, 138n30
Garroutte, Eva, 31
Gay Pride, 116
gender, 9, 26, 57, 100, 127n31; and bodily movement, 21, 42–43, 89–90, 104; in dance studies, 5; and embodiment, 49, 58–60, 62, 73; gendered violence, 15; gender roles, 104; performances of, 59, 89–90. *See also* femininity; feminism
gender studies, 58
geography, 9, 125
Georgia, 101
gesture, 5, 41, 63–64, 104, 110, 118
Giard, Luce, 91
Gibson, James J., 10, 14, 17–19, 21, 32, 34, 36–37, 41–43, 136n4, 137n8
ginga, 63–64
Glenberg, Arthur, 84–85
Glissant, Édouard, 8
Goeman, Mishuana, 22, 30
Goenpul people, 131n37
Google, 44
Gottschild, Brenda Dixon, 66
Great Britain, 27, 33, 122, 126n2; British colo-

nialism, 134n45. *See also* England; United Kingdom
grid, 13, 25–27, 67, 75
Griffith Park, 15
Grosfoguel, Ramón, 2, 49, 73
guest *(kuuyam)*, 29, 123n1
Gutierrez, Vicenta, 95

habitus, 42, 62–63, 101–2, 104, 127n28
Haig-Brown, Celia, 125, 125n28
Haitian Vodun, 63, 116
haka, 119
Hammergren, Lena, 127n31
Haraway, Donna, 7, 58
Harding, Sandra, 58
Harjo, Laura, 39
Harrington, J. P., 95
Haudenosaunee people, 7
Hauʻofa, Epeli, 8
heads, 4, 27–28, 71, 76, 96, 109, 111–12, 122; and dance, 63, 66, 119; and knowing, 51–53; and thinking, 1
Heisenberg, Werner, 46
heteropatriarchy, 26, 101
Hidatsa people, 94
hip-hop, 104
Hispanic people, 100
Hodson, Millicent, 136n28
Hokowhitu, Brendan, 39, 53, 129n7
hold, the 125n27
Hollywood Hills, 9, 126n4
Howe, LeAnne, 136n30
Hunkpapa Lakota people, 119
Husserl, Edmund, 32

Illinois: Chicago, 21, 96
immediacy, 39, 53, 113, 119, 129n7
implacement, 36, 40
Inconsolables (mountain range), 29, 126n4
India: Bangalore, 122
Indian Indenture Act (1850), 15
Indigenous and Native studies, 2, 6, 9–11, 37–38
Indonesian court dances, 88
information, 3, 50, 61, 74, 91, 99; and affordances, 84–85; and cognition, 81; and dance, 88–89, 102, 105, 109, 114; and knowing, 44–45; and perceiving, 10, 18, 45; visual, 27, 98; and walking, 17, 20, 28
Ingold, Tim, 27, 50, 126n2
Inquisition, 49, 73
Instagram, 117
intelligence, 17, 20, 43, 45–46, 81, 87, 108–9; morphological, 17, 81
interdependence, 40, 46, 116, 125n28
intra-action, 36, 40–41, 46, 123n2
islands, 8. *See also* archipelago as method
Israel-Palestine, 122
Italian people, 84, 122
Italy, 106

Jamaican people, 2, 131n39
James, C. L. R., 134n46
Jesuits, 84
Jewish people, 49, 73
Johnson, Imani Kai, 137n19
Johnson, Mark, 57

Kalpulli Yaocenoxtli, 119
Kant, Immanuel, 32
Kaschak, Michael P., 128n51
Khon, 88
Kim, Jina, 101
Kimmerer, Robin Wall, 47, 52, 123n2
kinestheme, 115, 138n36
kinesthesia, 10, 17–18, 32, 34, 56, 62, 70, 81, 89, 115–16, 127n31, 132
King, Tiffany Lethabo, 125n27
kinship, 3–5, 36–37, 45, 47, 52, 76, 137n16
Kirby, Vicki, 68
Kirkman-Harriman map (1860), 15
knowing, 88, 99, 129nn7–8, 131n36, 136n4; and acting/being, 36–55; and attention/attentiveness, 45, 68; and bodily movement, 2; and colonialism, 14, 64, 73–76; and connectedness, 9, 36–53; and dance, 63–68, 78–80, 90–95, 98, 104–6, 112–20; and decoloniality, 59, 71, 73–76, 80; embodied, 1–2, 4, 57–68; and information, 44–45; and locality, 129n2; and memory, 86; as movement, 2, 5–11; movement producing, 5; Native, 4–5; and walking, 14–18, 23, 28, 31–35, 121–22. *See also* epistemology

Krokos, Eric, 84
Kuruvungna Springs, 15

Lakoff, George, 57
land, 92, 99, 123n1; and archipelago as method, 8–9; and colonialism, 27–28, 30, 49–51, 59, 73–76, 131n39, 131n42; vs. Land, 16, 125n28; and locality, 129n2; repatriation of, 2, 124n7; responsibility to, 7
Land, 9, 33, 94; and being, 28–29, 75; Chumash Land, 14–15, 121, 126n4; and colonialism, 14–16, 26–27, 28–30, 51, 64; and connectedness, 45, 92, 125n28; definition, 125n28; and knowing, 43–46; and locality, 39, 44–45; as memory, 22, 30–31, 53; Paiute Land, 14, 16, 126n4; Palestinian Land, 128n43; responsibility to, 92; Tongva Land, 14, 64, 126n4; walking of, 19, 24–29
lang, k.d., 23
Las Casas, Bartolomé de, 131n39
Laurenti, Jean-Noël, 137n29
Lefebvre, Henri, 26, 127n22
Legat, Allice, 128n54
legs, 18, 27, 76, 98–99, 111, 114; and dance, 63, 100, 136n6; and walking, 20, 105
Lemhi Shoshone people, 94
Lepecki, André, 138n33
Lewis, Meriwether, 94
Liboiron, Max, 124nn7–8, 125n28, 128n48, 131n45
Lindy Hop, 104
Little Bear, Leroy, 130n32
location/locality, 28, 34, 49, 71, 129n2; and being, 36, 129n2; and dance, 88, 110, 137n29; definition, 36, 39; and Land, 39, 44–45; and memory, 14, 30, 82–83, 86; and place, 32, 41. *See also* land; Land
loci, 83–84
Locke, John, 51, 131n42
logocentrism, 58
Los Angeles Mission, 15
Los Angeles River, 26
Lovern, Lavonna, 101

Machuse, Lola, 79
Māori people, 39, 119, 129n7
Martin, Randy, 118, 138n36, 138n43

Martinican people, 8
Maryland, 68
Mason, William Marvin, 126n9
Mauss, Marcel, 90
McBeth, Sally, 94
McFee, Graham, 138n33
McMaster, Meryl, 97, 104, 112, 115
measurement, 17, 25, 42, 46, 52, 74–76, 104–8, 134n45; and disability, 21; and memory, 83–84; and space, 27, 30, 44, 51, 72
memory, 6, 68, 115; and affordances, 19, 34, 84–85; and archives, 10, 94–95; autobiographical, 78–79, 87–88, 93; cultural, 102; and dance, 10, 78–96, 117; and decoloniality, 93–96; decolonizing, 93–96; ecological remembering, 82–87; embodied, 9, 57–58; and facts, 78–79, 84–85, 87, 89; as fountain, 86–87, 89, 91–92; individual, 78–80; Land as, 22, 30–31, 53; and location/locality, 14, 30, 82–83, 86; memory palaces, 83–84, 86; misremembering, 85–86; muscle memory, 1, 89–90; and posture, 128n51; social, 78–80, 91; voluntary, 82; and walking, 9, 14, 29–31, 35, 83–85, 121
mental functions, 50, 56, 58, 79, 82, 86, 110, 132
Merleau-Ponty, Maurice, 32–33, 36–37, 41, 56, 130n13
Merritt, Michele, 123n4
Mexican Nahua people, 119
Mexican people, 2, 15
Michif people, 124n7
Michi Saagiig Nishnaabeg people, 4, 123n2
Middle Passage, 125n27
Midge, Tiffany, 119
mind-body dualism. *See* Cartesian dualism
Minich, Julie, 101
Minnesota: Minneapolis, 119
Miranda, Deborah, 95
mirror neurons, 116
mixed-ability dance, 115–16
modern dance, 65, 95, 103
Mohawk people, 125
monjeríos, 26
Moreton-Robinson, Aileen, 131n37
morphological intelligence, 17, 81
motion, 4, 40, 48, 51, 68, 76, 81, 130n32; and

affordances, 41; and being, 44, 54; and dance, 62–63, 66–67, 97, 103, 108, 112, 120; and disability, 20, 106; gendered, 21–22; and knowing, 45, 54, 120; and memory, 87, 90; and perceiving, 17–18, 34, 112; and walking, 35, 105

Mount San Jacinto, 15

movement, 4, 17, 27, 33, 43, 48, 61, 67, 69, 72, 137n19; and archipelago as method, 8; and connectedness, 3, 123n2; and dance, 3, 63, 65, 87–88, 93, 95–96, 102–20; gendered, 42–43; and knowing, 2, 5, 9, 32, 38, 41, 58–59, 73, 95; and memory, 78, 87–90; patterns of, 58, 60, 62–63, 68, 84–90, 102, 107, 116–17, 127n19, 135n9; producing knowing, 5; racialized, 22–24, 118, 125n27, 127n34

muscle memory, 1, 89–90

Mvskoke people, 39

National Forest Service, 16

Native knowing, 5–6, 7, 95, 104, 129n8

Native Lands, 14–16, 28–30, 45, 64, 75, 92, 121, 125n28, 126n4. *See also* Land

Native philosophy, 7, 37

Native research, 3

Native scholars, 3, 6, 7, 10–11, 28, 51, 123n2, 129n8. *See also individual nations and tribes*

Native studies. *See* Indigenous and Native studies

Navajo people, 64, 126n9

Nebraska, 117

neuromuscular system, 5, 17, 30, 68, 81, 116

neurophysiology, 9, 14

neuroscience, 3, 10

new materialism, 2, 9, 37, 129n8

New Mexico, 64

new morphology, 100, 136n6

New World, 50, 74, 131n39

New York City, 19, 60, 138n33

New Zealand, 97

Ngāti Pūkenga people, 39, 129n7

niches, 39, 42, 98–104, 111, 116, 130n30, 137n8

Nijinsky, Vaslav, 92; *Rite of Spring*, 136n28

North American Hand Talk, 118

North Carolina, 23

Northwest Coast First Nations people, 92

Obama, Barack, 23

objectivity, 34, 41, 47–48, 67, 76

Oceania, 8

Odissi, 88

ontology, 40. *See also* being

Opaskwayak Cree people, 3

Oregon, 7

Orientalism, 65

orientation, 7, 9, 12, 17, 27, 41–42, 61, 71, 81, 134n47, 135n9; and dance, 64, 66, 98; disorientation, 31; and knowing, 44–45, 58; reorientation, 20, 22, 101

Osage people, 38

Pacific Islands, 8. *See also* Oceania

Pairrebenne Trawlwoolway people, 3

Paiute Land, 14, 16, 126n4

Paiute people, 9

Pakistani British people, 33

Palestine, 122, 128n43

Palestinian Americans, 124n6

pantomime, 110

paths, 43, 85, 118; and walking, 13, 16–21, 24–26, 29, 35, 62

patriarchy, 42, 49, 73. *See also* heteropatriarchy; sexism

Pearce, Margaret W., 134n44

perceiving, 1, 36–37, 51–52, 56, 67–68, 71–72, 75, 132; and acting, 80, 111; and affordances, 10, 17–19, 22, 34, 42–46, 127n28; and archipelago as method, 8; and connectedness, 10–11, 35, 80; and dance, 3, 78, 96, 98–99, 104–8, 111–19; gendered, 21–23, 43; and implacement, 40; and information, 10, 18, 45; and knowing, 48, 54, 80, 136n4; of Land, 33; and memory, 84–89; and motion, 17–18, 34, 112; racialized, 22; and thinking, 5, 80–81; and walking, 20, 23, 31–32

performance, 10, 21, 33, 38, 60, 62–63, 71–72, 76, 78, 87; baroque, 92, 136n28; of dance, 64–66, 88–92, 97, 104, 107–10, 114–19; gendered, 59, 89–90; racialized, 29; and storytelling, 52–53

performance studies, 59

performativity, 40
Pfeifer, Rolf, 78, 82, 86, 91, 127n19, 135n12, 136n36
Phelan, Peggy, 138n33
phenomenology, 2–3, 9, 32–33, 35, 37, 41–42, 56–57, 99, 132; place-thought, 43
physicality, 40–41, 48, 68, 70–71, 99, 125n28, 130n35, 134n40; and affordances, 18, 21–22, 127n28; and colonialism, 75–76; and dance, 89, 92, 100, 103, 107, 110–12, 119; and intelligence, 81; and knowing, 1–2, 5, 9, 44; and locality, 39, 45; and memory, 91–92; and perception, 10; and practice, 60–61; relationship to mentality, 1; and thinking, 5; and walking, 9, 14, 24, 83
Piaget, Jean, 127n19
place, 39–41, 44, 47, 52, 54, 72–73, 125n28, 126n1; and archipelago as method, 8; and dance, 97, 102–4, 107–9, 112–20; and memory, 53, 57, 78–95; place-making, 2, 9, 13–35; Place-Thought, 36, 43, 53; vs. space, 9, 26, 49. *See also* displacement; emplacement; implacement
Plains Cree people, 97
plutocracy, 11
polka, 104
popular dance, 104
Porter, L. Archer, 117
Portuguese people, 50, 124n6
postmodern dance, 95
posture, 4, 24, 41, 68, 83, 104, 113, 128n51
Potawatomi people, 47, 123n2
proprioception, 2–3, 10, 17, 54, 72, 80, 83, 99, 108–9, 112–14, 116
Proust, Marcel, 82–83
Puerto Rican people, 2

Quandamooka First Nation, 131n37
queerness, 33
queer theory, 57
Quintilian, Marcus Fabius, 83

race, 12, 58, 63, 74, 100, 134n40; and affordances, 23, 128n35; and disability, 101; embodied, 22–24; and movement, 22–24, 118–19, 125n27, 127n34; and walking, 23–24

racism, 73, 123, 125n27
Raja, Vicente, 61, 88, 135n6
Red River Métis people, 124n7
relationality, 5, 10, 52–53, 131n37; vs. connectedness, 123n2
relationing, 17, 47, 123n2
Renaissance, 95
reorientation. *See* orientation
repertoire (Taylor), 60–61, 91
Ricci, Matteo, 84
Rifkin, Mary, 19, 22, 33
roads, 13, 18, 23, 25, 27, 35, 98, 105, 121, 128n43
rocks, 13, 19–20, 25, 29, 31, 34, 38–40, 43, 50, 85, 98–99, 105, 121, 125nn27–28
Rosa, Cristina, 63–64
Rose, Deborah Bird, 31, 53
Rosenfield, Israel, 85
Roy, Arundhati, 11

Sacagawea, 94–95
Saharafication, 29
samba de roda, 63
San Gabriel Mission, 15
San Gabriel Mountains, 15
Santa Ana River, 26
Santa Barbara Mission, 15
Scotland, 126n2
screen dance, 117
Sekimoto, Sachi, 22
Seneca people, 22
sensory-motor activity, 56, 57, 67, 96, 132, 135n7; and connectedness, 3; and information, 45, 85; and memory, 30, 79, 80–90; and race, 22
Sepulveda, Charles, 9, 26, 123n1
Sepúlveda, Juan Ginés de, 131n39
Serra, Junípero, 15
settler colonialism, 2, 5, 16, 28–29, 43–44, 49, 51, 58–59, 65, 95, 126n9. *See also* colonialism/imperialism
settler futurity, 16
settler-scholars, 7, 19, 21, 23, 27, 31, 36, 53, 57–58, 60, 64–65, 67–68, 99–101, 105, 117, 123n2, 123n5, 124nn6–7, 125n28, 126n2, 126n9, 127n31, 128n54, 138n33; definition, 124n8

sexism, 42, 73. *See also* patriarchy
sexual violence, 15, 95
Sharpe, Christina, 125n27
Shea Murphy, Jacqueline, 65, 123nn2–3, 124n16, 125n17, 125n30
Sheets-Johnstone, Maxine, 56, 59, 123n3, 135n7
Shehadesh, Raja, 128n43
Sheppard, Alice (Wheelchair Dancer), 97, 103, 105, 137n18
Shildrick, Margrit, 36–37, 40–41, 53
ship, the, 125n27
shoals, 125n27
Simpson, Leanne Betasamosake, 4–5, 12, 44–45, 48, 52, 54, 94–95, 121, 123n1, 124n11
situated knowledges, 58
Situationism, 23
slavery, 23, 125n27
slipping/tripping, 24, 31–32, 105, 129n60
Smithsonian Institution, 95
Sobchack, Vivian, 99–100, 102, 114–15
social dance, 110, 118
sociology, 9, 59, 65
Solnit, Rebecca, 23
South Africa, 118
Spain: Córdoba, 73; Spanish colonialism, 14–15, 26, 49–50, 65, 73, 126n4, 131n39; Spanish missions, 15–16, 26, 64, 95
speaking with names, 31, 53, 79–80, 86, 93
sports science, 84, 107
square dance, 16
Standing Rock Sioux people, 36, 119
steps, 44, 54, 75; in dance, 88, 93, 104–6, 109, 119, 137n29; in walking, 13, 17–20, 25, 28, 99, 127n22
stillness, 43, 48, 51, 74–76, 104, 120
storytelling, 5, 30–31, 52–54, 95, 103
studio classes, 1
Styres, Sandra, 125n28
Sweden, 122, 127n31
Sweet, Jill, 64

tacit knowledge, 91
tap dance, 88
Taylor, Diana, 60–61, 91
technique, 31, 68, 72, 74–75, 83–84, 90, 108, 136n6

Tewa people, 28, 64–66
Texas, 100–101
thinking, 36, 38–39, 54, 66, 75, 111, 118, 123n5, 129n3; archipelagic, 8; and connectedness, 3; embodied, 1, 5, 17, 57–60, 72–73; and knowing, 50; and Land, 43; and memory, 57, 84–86, 93; and moving, 5, 80–81, 95, 123n4; and perceiving, 5, 80–81; and space, 27; speculative, 93; and writing, 71
Thompson, Evan, 56, 58, 132, 135n6, 135n9
TikTok, 117
Tinker, George "Tink," 38, 40, 129n4
Tłı̨chǫ Déné people, 31
Tongo, 8
Tongva Land, 14, 64, 126n4
Tongva people, 9, 15–16, 29, 64, 123n1
training, 39, 61, 89, 94, 106–8, 110, 113, 115, 130n30
transhumance, 23
truth, 44, 93, 124n8
Tsimshian people, 92
Tuck, Eve, 16, 28, 124n7
Turtle Dances, 116
twerking, 119
twist (dance), 104
Tynan, Lauren, 3

Ukraine, 122
Unangax̂ people, 16
United Kingdom, 97. *See also* England; Great Britain
University of Chicago, 96
urban studies, 9

van Dooren, Thom, 31, 53
Vergunst, Jo Lee, 126n2, 127n22, 129n60
violence, 11, 14–15, 23, 38, 49, 51, 76, 94. *See also* ableism; colonialism/imperialism; displacement; patriarchy; racism; sexual violence; slavery
voguing, 119

Wacquant, Loïc, 67
wake, the, 125n27
walking, 10, 12, 41–44, 54, 69, 72, 75–76, 90, 98–99, 105, 121–22, 126n2, 126n4, 127n31;

Index · 161

walking (*continued*)
  and affordances, 14, 19–20, 23–25, 28–29, 31, 35; and attention/attentiveness, 13–14, 20, 25–26, 29, 32; and knowing, 14–18, 23, 28, 31–35, 121–22; and memory, 9, 14, 29–31, 35, 83–85, 121; paths for, 13, 16–21, 24–26, 29, 35, 62; and perceiving, 20, 23, 31–32; as place-making, 13–35; racialized, 23–24; and rhythm, 127n22; and slipping/tripping, 24, 31–32, 105, 129n60
walking sticks, 20, 24, 121
waltz, 104
Washington, DC, 105
Watts, Vanessa, 7, 36–37, 39–40, 43, 51, 53, 121
Watts Belser, Julia, 105
weather, the, 125n27
Weighill, Tharon, 15, 65, 80
Weingourt, Gilbert, 122
Weingourt, Rita, 122
Westcott, Kathleen, 31

Western Apache people, 31, 53, 79, 80, 86, 93–94
Wheelchair Dancer. *See* Sheppard, Alice (Wheelchair Dancer)
wheelchairs, 9, 20, 24, 97, 99–100, 103, 105–6, 112, 115
whiteness, 5, 11, 21, 23–24, 29, 58, 97, 118, 124n15
whole-bodied-ness, 45
whole body intelligence, 45
Wilson, Shawn, 3
Wind River Shoshone people, 94
Wynter, Sylvia, 2, 74–75, 131n39, 134n46, 134nn40–41

Yang, K. Wayne, 16, 28, 124n7
yoga, 65, 89, 113
Young, Iris Marion, 21–22, 34, 42, 57, 102

Zwaan, Rolf A., 128n51

www.ingramcontent.com/pod-product-compliance
Lightning Source LLC
Chambersburg PA
CBHW031320160426
43196CB00007B/605